Photo by Susan Johann

A scene from the Signature Theatre Company production of "Talking Pictures." Set design

TALKING PICTURES

BY HORTON FOOTE

★

DRAMATISTS
PLAY SERVICE
INC.

2

TALKING PICTURES was produced at Signature Theatre Company (James Houghton, Artistic Director; Thomas C. Proehl, Managing Director; Elliot Fox, Associate Director) in New York City, on September 23, 1994. It was directed by Carol Goodheart; the set design was by Colin D. Young; the costume design was by Teresa Snider-Stein and Jonathan Green; the lighting design was by Jeffrey S. Koger and the production stage manager was Bethany Ford. The cast was as follows:

KATIE BELL JACKSON .... Samantha Reynolds
VESTA JACKSON .... Sarah Paulson
MYRA TOLLIVER .... Hallie Foote
MR. JACKSON .... Frank Girardeau
MRS. JACKSON .... Alice McLane
WILLIS .... Seth Jones
ESTAQUIO TREVINO .... Isaiah G. Cazares
PETE .... Eddie Kaye Thomas
GLADYS .... Susan Wands
ASHENBACK .... Ed Hodson
GERARD ANDERSON .... Kenneth Cavett

3

CHARACTERS

KATIE BELL JACKSON
VESTA JACKSON
MYRA TOLLIVER
MR. JACKSON
MRS. JACKSON
WILLIS
ESTAQUIO TREVINO
PETE
GLADYS
ASHENBACK
GERARD ANDERSON

PLACE

Harrison, Texas
1929

4

TALKING PICTURES

ACT ONE

A living room, bedroom, porch and a portion of the yard of the Jackson house in Harrison, Texas. It has very small rooms, a small parlour and yard. Katie Bell Jackson, 16, is reading a book in the living room. Her sister, Vesta, 18, is eating popcorn.

KATIE BELL.   Sister, come give me some popcorn.

VESTA.   No. Go out in the kitchen and get your own.

KATIE BELL.   Selfish!

VESTA.   Selfish, yourself. *(Myra Tolliver, 34, comes into the house looking down at a run in her stockings.)* What's the matter?

MYRA.   I've got a run in my stocking. Brand new, too. *(She goes into her room and takes off the stocking.)*

KATIE BELL.   How was the picture show this afternoon?

MYRA.   Pretty fair.

VESTA.   *(Calling to Myra.)* Was it hot walking from town?

MYRA.   Yes. And dusty.

KATIE BELL.   *(Calling to Myra.)* Who was in that picture show?

MYRA.   Bessie Love. *(She has changed stockings and begins to darn stockings. Katie Bell and Vesta go into Myra's room.)*

VESTA.   Who?

MYRA.   Bessie Love. What are you reading, Katie Bell?

KATIE BELL.   *Ben Hur.*

MYRA.   Oh, that was a wonderful movie.

KATIE BELL.   It looks like it. There are scenes from the movie in the book. Were you playing the piano for the picture show when you saw it?

MYRA.   Yes, I was.

KATIE BELL.   Ramon Navarro was in the movie, wasn't he?

MYRA. Yes, and Frances X. Bushman.

KATIE BELL. Was the movie like the book?

MYRA. I don't know. I never read the book.

KATIE BELL. Is Ramon Navarro very handsome?

MYRA. I think so.

VESTA. He's a Mexican.

KATIE BELL. No, he's not.

VESTA. Yes, he is too.

KATIE BELL. Is he, Miss Myra?

MYRA. Yes, he is. And he's very worried, I read.

KATIE BELL. Why?

MYRA. What will happen to his career when the movies are all talkies.

KATIE BELL. Why does that worry him?

VESTA. Because he talks Mexican, goose. Once people hear him talk Mexican they'll all know he's not American.

KATIE BELL. Can't he learn to speak English? I saw a Mexican boy up town the other day and I asked him his name and he said it was Estaquio Trevino and he spoke English just as plain as anybody.

VESTA. Katie Bell Jackson, were you talking to a Mexican? Mama would have a fit if she knew.

KATIE BELL. I wasn't talking to him. I just asked him his name.

VESTA. You mean you walked right up to a strange Mexican and asked him his name?

KATIE BELL. No, I didn't go right up to anybody. Sally Meyers and I were walking down the street and he came up to us and asked us if there were any other Mexicans here and Sally said yes, there were some across the track and I said yes that was true and he said enough to start a church?

VESTA. Enough to start a church?

KATIE BELL. That's what he said.

VESTA. Why did he say that?

KATIE BELL. I don't know. I didn't ask him and then he asked us our name and we told him.

VESTA. You told him? You told a Mexican boy your name?

KATIE BELL. Yes.

6

VESTA. Sister, I am shocked. Then what happened ...

KATIE BELL. And then we asked him his name, and a colored boy walked by and he asked if there were many colored people here and I said as many as there are white, and Sally said she thought more, and then we bid him goodbye and walked on. *(Myra leaves her room and goes to the piano in the living room and starts to look over sheet music. Vesta and Katie Bell follow after her.)*

VESTA. Myra, Mama says in exchange for part of your rent you are going to give Katie Bell and me music lessons —

MYRA. Yes.

VESTA. Mama says after I learn to play the piano, I can take organ lessons so I can play for the church on Sunday. *(Katie Bell makes a face.)* Why are you making a face?

KATIE BELL. Because I don't ever want to play an organ in church or anywhere. I want to play the piano for picture shows like Myra.

VESTA. I'd like to hear you tell Mama that.

KATIE BELL. I'm not about to tell Mama that. *(Myra goes back to her room with sheet music.)*

MYRA. *(Calling out to the girls.)* Well, honey, don't ever think about playing piano in picture shows. Those days are about over, I fear. I think the Queen here is about one of the last of the silent theaters. Mr. Santos says he will keep it that way as long as he can, as he doesn't care for the talkies, but I don't think he can hold out much longer. The theaters in El Campo, Bay City and Richmond have all gone talkie, and I hear Eagle Lake and Columbus are about to. Why, I read the other day in some movie magazine or other where they may stop making silent pictures all together. *(Katie Bell and Vesta have remained in the living room.)*

KATIE BELL. Miss Myra has seen a talking picture. She saw it in Houston when she took Pete in to stay with his Daddy. I wish I could see a talking picture.

VESTA. Well, you're never going to get to so just get over wishing that. You've never seen a silent movie.

KATIE BELL. Well, neither have you — Anyway, Miss Myra tells me the stories of all the movies she sees and she tells

7

them so wonderfully I feel like I've seen them.

VESTA.   Does Mama know she tells you the stories of all those pictures?

KATIE BELL.   No.

VESTA.   Well, I bet she would have a fit if she knew. *(A pause.)* Did she tell you the story of that talking picture she saw in Houston?

KATIE BELL.   Yes. She did.

VESTA.   Was it a love story? *(Katie Bell and Vesta go back into Myra's room.)*

KATIE BELL.   Miss Myra, was that talking picture you saw in Houston a love story?

MYRA.   No, not really. Well, now I don't know. It was a love story, I suppose, but an unconventional one. It was the story of the love of a father for his son.

VESTA.   What was the name of it?

MYRA.   *The Singing Fool.*

KATIE BELL.   Would you tell the story to Vesta? She's never heard you tell the story of a picture show and I told her ...

MYRA.   You tell the story to Vesta —

KATIE BELL.   Oh, I can't.

MYRA.   Sure, you can. Tell it like I told it to you.

KATIE BELL.   I can't remember it all.

MYRA.   Sure you can.

KATIE BELL.   I remember there was this man and he was a famous singer and he was married. Is that right?

MYRA.   Yes, that's right.

KATIE BELL.   And they had a little boy and he loved his little boy very much, but then he and his wife were separated and one night when he was to sing his little boy got sick and died. But he had to go on stage and sing anyway, even though his heart was breaking.

VESTA.   That's sad.

KATIE BELL.   Of course, it's sad. Miss Myra said everybody in the picture show was crying. Didn't you?

MYRA.   Yes.

VESTA.   Were you crying?

MYRA.   Oh, yes. Like a baby.

8

KATIE BELL.   Sing that song for Vesta.

MYRA.   *(Singing.)*
          "FRIENDS MAY FORSAKE US
          LET THEM ALL FORSAKE US
          I STILL HAVE YOU, SONNY BOY.
          YOU CAME FROM HEAVEN
          AND I KNOW YOUR WORTH,
          YOU MADE A HEAVEN FOR ME RIGHT
               HERE ON EARTH.
          BUT THE ANGELS THEY GOT LONELY
          AND THEY TOOK YOU BECAUSE THEY WERE
               LONELY
          NOW I'M LONELY, TOO, SONNY BOY."*

VESTA.   Did the little boy die?

MYRA.   Yes.

KATIE BELL.   And the father had to go and sing that song even though his heart was breaking.

VESTA.   Oh, that's so sad. It's like the story Brother Meyers told in church the other night about this poor widow who had no money and no job.

KATIE BELL.   Didn't she have a husband?

VESTA.   No, goose. Didn't you hear me say she was a widow? Widows don't have husbands. If you're a widow your husband is dead. And if you're a grass widow your husband is alive and you're divorced. Myra is a grass widow.

KATIE BELL.   Are you?

MYRA.   Yes. *(Vesta goes into the living room. Katie Bell follows her.)*

KATIE BELL.   What did that woman's husband die of?

VESTA.   What woman?

KATIE BELL.   The one Brother Meyers told you about.

VESTA.   Good heavens, I don't know that. Ask Brother Meyers.

KATIE BELL.   Is that the whole story?

VESTA.   No, there's more to it.

KATIE BELL.   Well, what's the rest of it?

* See Special Note on Music on copyright page.

VESTA.   Well, she was desperate because she had starving children and everything ...

KATIE BELL.   And what happened?

VESTA.   Well, if you'll be quiet for five minutes I'll tell you.

KATIE BELL.   I know what happened. She prayed to God and he saved them.

VESTA.   How did you know that?

KATIE BELL.   Because that's what always happens when Brother Meyers tells a story.

VESTA.   *(Calling to Myra.)* What was the name of that talking picture you saw?

MYRA.   *The Singing Fool. (Mr. Jackson, 45, in overalls, carrying a lunch pail comes in. A soft spoken, sad man.)*

MR. JACKSON.   Hello.

VESTA.   Hello, Daddy.

KATIE BELL.   Hello, Daddy.

MYRA.   *(Calling from her room.)* Hello, Mr. Jackson.

KATIE BELL.   *(Calling to Myra.)* Daddy got bumped.

MYRA.   *(Calling from her room.)* I know I heard, I'm so sorry.

MR. JACKSON.   Well, it's not the end of the world. I still have a job.

VESTA.   Who bumped you Daddy?

MR. JACKSON.   Someone with more seniority than I have that wanted my job here.

KATIE BELL.   Now Daddy's going to have to bump somebody — We're going over to Cuero on his day off to look it over and if he likes it, he'll bump the man that works there, and we'll all go live in Cuero. When are we going to Cuero, Daddy, if we go?

MR. JACKSON.   Well, we have to try and sell our house, see if we can't find a place to live there.

KATIE BELL.   *(Calling to Myra.)* Have you ever been to Cuero, Miss Myra?

MYRA.   *(Calling from her room.)* Yes, I've played in the picture house there.

KATIE BELL.   *(Calling to Myra.)* Is it a nice town?

MYRA.   *(Calling from her room.)* I think so.

VESTA.   *(Calling to Myra.)* As nice as here?

MYRA. *(Calling from her room.)* I like it here better —

VESTA. Oh, Daddy, if we move to Cuero in six weeks I better start my piano lessons with Myra right away, if she's going to teach me.

MR. JACKSON. Well, that's up to you and your Mama.

VESTA. *(Calling to Myra.)* Can you start teaching me right away?

MYRA. *(Calling from her room.)* Why, yes, I don't see why not.

VESTA. Oh, grand.

MR. JACKSON. Where is your Mama?

VESTA. She's at the Missionary Society.

MR. JACKSON. I'm going across the road to work in my garden while it's still light. *(He starts out — he pauses. He goes to the door of Myra's room.)* Your boy coming here today, Myra?

MYRA. Yes, I'm waiting for him now.

MR. JACKSON. How long has he been in Houston?

MYRA. Two weeks.

MR. JACKSON. Two weeks? Doesn't seem possible. Staying with his father?

MYRA. Yes.

MR. JACKSON. Is he married again?

MYRA. Yes.

MR. JACKSON. Does he have any other children?

MYRA. Yes, two. Both boys.

MR. JACKSON. Where did you come from Myra?

MYRA. I was born and raised in Nacogdoches.

MR. JACKSON. Oh yes. I remember now. Mrs. Jackson told me that. I used to have a run through Nacogdoches.

MYRA. Did you?

MR. JACKSON. That was the run I had before I came to Harrison. *(Mrs. Jackson enters the living room through the front door.)*

MRS. JACKSON. Well, Daddy, you beat me home.

MR. JACKSON. Yes, I did. How was the Missionary Society?

MRS. JACKSON. Oh, I tell you the sorrow in this world. You don't know when you are blessed. Mrs. Davis was with us today telling us about the missionaries among the leper colonies. Oh, the tales of those lepers are harrowing. Brother

Meyers is going to preach a whole sermon about the lepers on Sunday, he says.

MR. JACKSON. I thought Mrs. Davis was a Presbyterian.

MRS. JACKSON. She is.

MR. JACKSON. Then why was she at the Methodist Missionary Society?

MRS. JACKSON. To get us all interested in the leper work. She says it's interdenominational. Brother Meyers agrees. He prayed so beautifully about it. I just love to hear Brother Meyers pray — Well, I'd better get supper started.

MR. JACKSON. And I'm going out to my garden. *(He exits. Mrs. Jackson goes to the door to Myra's room.)*

MRS. JACKSON. Your boy not home yet, Myra?

MYRA. No, I'm expecting him any second now.

VESTA. Mama, may I start my piano lessons right away with Myra. Daddy says we may be moving to Cuero pretty soon.

MRS. JACKSON. We'll discuss that later. *(She starts out.)*

VESTA. I'll help you, Mama. *(They leave. Katie Bell goes into Myra's room.)*

KATIE BELL. If I tell you a secret will you swear not to tell anybody?

MYRA. Yes, I swear.

KATIE BELL. Two years ago when I was in El Campo visiting Sarah Lundy we slipped into the picture show over there. We saw Clara Bow in *Rough House Rosie*. Did you see that?

MYRA. Yes, I did.

KATIE BELL. How many picture shows have you seen?

MYRA. Oh, hundreds —

KATIE BELL. How long have you been playing the piano at picture shows?

MYRA. Let's see. About eleven years.

KATIE BELL. What made you come here?

MYRA. Because they were looking for someone to play the piano at the Queen.

KATIE BELL. What was the best picture show you ever saw? *(Myra goes into the living room and to the piano. She takes more sheet music. Katie Bell follows her.)*

MYRA. Oh, heavens ... I'll have to think about that.

KATIE BELL. Who is your favorite actor?

MYRA. I'll have to think about that, too. *(A pause.)* I think *Romona* with Dolores Del Rio was one of my favorite pictures.

KATIE BELL. She's Mexican, too, isn't she?

MYRA. Yes —

KATIE BELL. Are there any other Mexican movie stars?

MYRA. Yes. Lupe Velez, Antonio Moreno.

KATIE BELL. They're movie stars?

MYRA. Yes. *(She goes back into her room. She gets her purse, gloves and hat. Katie Bell follows.)*

KATIE BELL. How do you get to be a movie star?

MYRA. Oh, I don't know.

KATIE BELL. Are there only Mexican and American movie stars?

MYRA. No. There are Russian and German and Italian and English and Polish —

KATIE BELL. Movie stars?

MYRA. Yes.

KATIE BELL. How much money does a movie star make?

MYRA. Depends on the movie star. *(She has her hat and gloves on. She goes again into the living room. Katie Bell follows.)*

KATIE BELL. They're all rich aren't they?

MYRA. Pretty rich. Richer than I am certainly. *(Mrs. Jackson enters.)*

MRS. JACKSON. Katie Bell, come in and help your sister, please. *(She and Katie Bell exit for the kitchen. Myra goes outside to the porch, sits on the steps. Willis enters.)*

WILLIS. Hi —

MYRA. Hello.

WILLIS. Pete home yet?

MYRA. No. How was work?

WILLIS. Hot. I'm tired. Laying bricks in the hot sun is not my idea of a classy job. *(A pause.)* Well, beggars can't be choosers.

MYRA. Is your room over the garage hot?

WILLIS. Like an oven. How is your room?

MYRA. It gets pretty hot.

WILLIS. A little breeze now.

MYRA. Yes.

WILLIS.   How about a date Sunday night after the picture show?

MYRA.   Don't you have to get up early Monday morning?

WILLIS.   Five o'clock. Same as usual.

MYRA.   Willis, you'll be dead if we go on having dates at night and your having to get up for work so early. Anyway, where can we go at ten o'clock at night, but the ice cream parlour and it closes at eleven and they just sigh when we come in at ten as if to say I hope you won't loiter.

WILLIS.   When else can I see you? You work at the picture show every afternoon and every night, seven days a week. I wanted a date tonight, but you said you thought you should come back since it was Pete's first night home. *(Katie Bell comes to the door.)*

KATIE BELL.   Phone, Myra —

MYRA.   Excuse me — *(She goes into the house. Katie Bell comes outside.)*

KATIE BELL.   Did you ever see a talking picture?

WILLIS.   I saw one in Houston that was partly talking.

KATIE BELL.   How do they get those pictures to talk?

WILLIS.   Beats me.

KATIE BELL.   Are you a Baptist?

WILLIS.   Born and bred.

KATIE BELL.   Someone said you were. We're Methodists. Myra is Methodist, too. Can Baptists and Methodists marry?

WILLIS.   They can if they want to.

KATIE BELL.   Vesta was about to date a Baptist boy, but Mama discouraged it. She says mixed marriages are not a very good idea. It's very confusing to the children. With the father going to one church and the mother to another. Now my father doesn't go to any church and that worries my mother considerable. Of course, like Mama says, he is the best man that ever walked this earth, but still. *(A pause.)* Do you think people that attend picture shows are going to Hell?

WILLIS.   No, I don't.

KATIE BELL.   I don't either. Brother Meyers says if they go on weekdays they are liable to go and if they go on Sundays they are bound to. I certainly don't think Myra is going to Hell, do you?

WILLIS. No.

KATIE BELL. Anyway, she has to go. It's her job. *(Myra comes back out.)* Willis says you're not going to Hell if you go to the picture shows.

MYRA. I wasn't worried. Thank you anyway, Willis, for telling me. That was Pete's Daddy on the phone. He said Pete wanted to know if he could stay another day — I said, yes. Well, it's time for me to go to work. See you all later. *(She goes.)*

KATIE BELL. She had been crying. Couldn't you tell?

WILLIS. No.

KATIE BELL. Well, she had. I can tell. She cries all the time, too, in her room when Pete isn't there. I guess she doesn't think we can hear her, but we can. Papa says she's worried over losing her job at the picture show. He says she has lots to worry her, says it's hard having to raise a boy by herself. I think she's pretty, don't you?

WILLIS. Yes, I do. *(Mrs. Jackson comes to the door.)*

MRS. JACKSON. Katie Bell, come here, please.

KATIE BELL. Yes, Ma'am. *(She goes to her mother.)*

MRS. JACKSON. What's all this about some little boy dying at the picture show. Vesta's all upset about it.

KATIE BELL. He didn't die at the picture show, Mama. He died in the picture show.

MRS. JACKSON. Oh, is that how it was. I thought some little boy died at the picture show here.

KATIE BELL. No, he died in a picture show in Houston.

MRS. JACKSON. It seems to me you are awfully interested in picture shows all of a sudden.

KATIE BELL. No, Ma'am. Just interested in the stories, Mama. *(A pause.)* Mama —

MRS. JACKSON. What?

KATIE BELL. Do you think that people that go to picture shows will go to Hell, especially if they go on Sundays?

MRS. JACKSON. No, I don't. Not that I would go myself and I don't want you or your sister ever going. *(A pause.)* I

15

went to a tent show once.

KATIE BELL. You did?

MRS. JACKSON. Yes, and a medicine show, too. I didn't care too much for either of them, but I don't think I'm going to Hell, because I went. That's just Brother Meyers talking. He's a good man, but extreme in his views. How are you, Willis?

WILLIS. Pretty fair, thank you.

MRS. JACKSON. Hot enough for you?

WILLIS. Oh, yes. *(He starts out.)* See you all later. *(He goes.)*

KATIE BELL. Mama?

MRS. JACKSON. Yes.

KATIE BELL. I think he is courting Miss Myra, don't you?

MRS. JACKSON. It seems. He's over here a lot.

KATIE BELL. I think he's nice, don't you?

MRS. JACKSON. Yes, I do. And I think Myra is nice, too.

KATIE BELL. Pete isn't coming home today.

MRS. JACKSON. Oh.

KATIE BELL. When she came out to tell us that I think she'd been crying.

MRS. JACKSON. She's very emotional. I think it's seeing all those picture shows.

KATIE BELL. Papa says it's not, he says —

MRS. JACKSON. *(Interrupting.)* I know what he says, but your Papa isn't the final authority on everything. Just think how hearing the story of one of those picture shows upset your sister, what if you watched as many as she does — why I think you'd be upset all the time.

KATIE BELL. Mama, do you know any Mexicans?

MRS. JACKSON. Good Lord, no. Why would I know any Mexicans? You're the strangest child I ever saw. Never know what you're going to worry me with next. Moving picture shows and now Mexicans. *(She goes in the house. Katie Bell follows as the light fades. The lights are brought up — later that evening. Willis is sitting on the Jackson steps. Katie Bell and Vesta enter in the living room. Katie Bell turns on the radio. She gets classical music. Myra comes into the yard.)*

WILLIS. Good evening.

MYRA. Sh. Mr. Jackson's asleep. He goes to bed by eight-thirty or nine. He's up at four. He takes his train at five.

WILLIS. I know. There are lights on in the house though.

MYRA. That's the girls in the living room listening to the radio.

WILLIS. They let them listen to the radio, but not go to the picture show?

MYRA. They can only listen to programs of classical music. Jessica Dragonette, the Firestone Hour, Lawrence Tibbett. Once Mrs. Jackson caught Katie Bell listening to Rudy Vallee and she threatened to throw the radio out the window.

WILLIS. The Joplins have a radio. They invited me over the other night to listen to a boxing match.

MYRA. Did you go?

WILLIS. Oh, yes.

MYRA. Why aren't you in bed asleep?

WILLIS. It's very close in my room tonight.

MYRA. You should have a fan.

WILLIS. I know, I'm going to get one. Do you have a fan?

MYRA. No.

WILLIS. I bet your room is hot too?

MYRA. Terrible.

WILLIS. I'd say let's walk back to town and get some ice cream but I think the drug store would be closed by the time we got there.

MYRA. Yes, it would. Anyway, I'm too tired tonight to walk another step.

WILLIS. Why were you so late getting home tonight?

MYRA. Sue Jessie had to leave early because of some kind of going on at the Eastern Star, so I told her I would total up the ticket sales for her. She sells the tickets, you see, and she's always worrying she'll come out short. Anyway, it took me longer than I thought to get it all straight so Sue Jessie wouldn't have a breakdown when she comes tomorrow. And then I went for a walk.

WILLIS. By yourself?

MYRA. Yes, sir —

WILLIS. Myra, don't be walking around by yourself this time of night. *(Inside, Katie Bell changes the radio station to dance mu-*

sic.) It's not safe.

VESTA.   Katie Bell Jackson, what are you doing? That's dance music! Mama would have a fit if she knew you were listening to dance music! Turn that off and come to bed! *(Katie Bell turns off the radio. She and Vesta exit.)*

WILLIS.   Myra —

MYRA.   What?

WILLIS.   Were you crying today?

MYRA.   When?

WILLIS.   Right after you talked to your husband.

MYRA.   My ex-husband. I was crying. *(A pause.)* My ex-husband can be so insensitive sometimes. After I gave my permission for Pete to stay he said right out that Pete didn't want to live with me any longer. He said he wanted to stay in Houston with him and his wife and his boys all the time.

WILLIS.   What is his name?

MYRA.   Whose?

WILLIS.   Your ex-husband's?

MYRA.   Gerard. Gerard Anderson. His new wife's name is Jacqueline Kate. They call her Jackie Kate.

WILLIS.   Would you let Pete live permanently in Houston?

MYRA.   No, he's just making the whole thing up to get at me. I said to him why don't you leave me alone, stop tormenting me. The courts have given Pete to me except for two weeks in the summertime. He said, it wasn't his doing, Pete doesn't want to come back, well, I said, put Pete on the phone and let him tell me that. He's in the pool swimming, he says, in our swimming pool. Do you have even a public swimming pool in Harrison, he said? No, I said we don't, we do have the river which Pete is not allowed to go in because of snakes, alligators, and suckholes. That's what you think, he says. He goes into that river all the time, sneaking, he said, while you're busy playing the piano at the picture show. Well, listen, I said, that's the way I put a roof over our head and food on the table by playing at the picture show. Then he said, in a very sarcastic way, I hear you may lose your job at the picture show to the talking pictures. How are you going to support a four-teen-year-old boy if that happens, he said, don't you worry about me, I said, I'll get a job. I always have. And I have, too. When we divorced I didn't have a dime and he was working in construction then and barely making anything and so I knew I couldn't count on him for any kind of support, and I didn't want to take anything from him even if I could — And so it was up to me to always take care of Pete and myself from then on. Oh, he sent Pete five dollars at Christmas and on his birthday, but that's all. He'd been drinking, you know.

WILLIS.   Does he drink?

MYRA.   He sure does, all the time these days.

WILLIS.   I don't drink.

MYRA.   I know you don't.

WILLIS.   My Daddy drank something fierce. The sight of him cured me once and for all. Is that why you left him because he drank?

MYRA.   No, he didn't drink then.

WILLIS.   Why did you separate?

MYRA.   Oh, Lord. I don't know really. I've asked myself that a million times, to tell you the truth. We started going together back in High School.

WILLIS.   Nacogdoches?

MYRA.   Yes. *(A pause.)* I guess you might say we just outgrew each other. My Daddy said if I left him he'd never speak to me again and he didn't until the day he died and then he just barely nodded to me when I went into his room. But Gerard and I thought it was the best thing to do at the time. A year after the divorce he came over where I was living with Pete and asked me to marry him again. But by then I had my first job at a picture show and was supporting myself and Pete. *(A pause.)* Gerard's a contractor now. He's a rich man, he tells me and Pete says he thinks he is. He has a car and a truck and a swimming pool and a two story house and a new wife and two more sons — *(A pause.)* Of course, I've never regretted leaving him. He wasn't mean to me, he never hit me or yelled at me — but he never stayed home except to eat and sleep. I don't think he was running around with other women and he wasn't drinking then, but he just never stayed home. I had Pete the first year we were married, and he'd say, come on and bring the baby, where to, I'd say, the domino parlour or the pool hall? I can't bring a baby to a domino parlour or a pool hall, I'd tell him. Do you mind if I go, he'd say, no, I would always say, go on, I don't mind. I got lonesome, of course. *(A pause. She sings half to herself.)* "When there are gray skies. I don't mind the gray skies."*

WILLIS.   I hope to be rich one day.

MYRA.   Well, I hope you are for your sake. If that's what you want. And if it brings you happiness — *(She sings again to herself.)* "The angels, they grew lonely —"*

WILLIS.   What's that song? I never heard it before.

MYRA.   It's a song they sang in that picture show I saw in Houston.

WILLIS.   Was it a talking picture?

MYRA.   Yes.

WILLIS.   What was it called?

MYRA.   *The Singing Fool,* with Al Jolson.

WILLIS.   Oh, yes. I saw him in *The Jazz Singer.* Did you see that?

MYRA.   No.

WILLIS.   That wasn't all talking. That was part talking and part silent. He sang "Mammy" in that one. He wore black face when he sang it.

MYRA.   He wore black face in this one, too.

WILLIS.   When he sang?

MYRA.   Yes.

WILLIS.   I wonder why he does that?

MYRA.   I don't know.

WILLIS.   You've been here a year, Myra?

MYRA.   Yes, and before that Flatonia and before that —

WILLIS.   Were you always playing the piano in picture shows?

MYRA.   Yes.

WILLIS.   Did you ever think of marrying again?

MYRA.   Once. A man in Lufkin, Harold Menefee. I almost married him, but Pete didn't like him and I don't think he

* See Special Note on Music on copyright page.

liked Pete, though he swore he did and I was afraid he might not be good to Pete after we married, so I said no.

WILLIS.   I like Pete.

MYRA.   I'm glad.

WILLIS.   Does he like me?

MYRA.   I don't know, I've never asked him.

WILLIS.   We played catch together the night before he went to visit his Daddy.

MYRA.   I know you did.

WILLIS.   I bought a glove just so I could play with him — I want to play with him a lot when he gets back. My youngest brother is sixteen and I play catch a lot with him when I go back home.

MYRA.   It's not easy, you know living in a rented room in somebody else's house with a fourteen-year-old boy. I dream some day of having my own house with a room for myself and a room for Pete. *(A pause.)* It's a pretty night, isn't it?

WILLIS.   Yes. *(A pause.)* I had some good news tonight.

MYRA.   What?

WILLIS.   Mr. Charlie called me into his house tonight after supper and he said his business had improved a lot and that he was very pleased with my work and that he has had contracts for four more houses and I could count on steady work and a raise in pay. I told him that was certainly good news because I was trying to make some plans of my own, what kind of plans he asked, and I said, personal plans. *(A pause.)* I don't know what you think about me exactly, but I think you're a mighty fine person. I have my eye on a small lot and now that I know I'll have a steady job and a raise in pay I can see my way clear on making an offer on the lot and if I can get it at a price I can afford, I could start building a house. Mr. Charlie said he would help me every Sunday after church. It would be a small house, of course, and it wouldn't have a swimming pool. Anyway, like I said, I don't know what you think about me, but I think highly of you. *(A pause.)* Of course, I don't know if you remembered my telling you I was married before, too.

MYRA.   Yes, I remember you telling me that.

WILLIS.   We had no children, my wife left me for another man two years after we were married. That hurt a lot, of course, because I won't lie to you, I was sure crazy about her. And I thought the sun rose and set on her. And I swore to myself at the time I would never marry again, it shook me up so. That was five years ago, of course, and I only think of Gladys once in a while now, like when she sends me a postcard from New Orleans or Galveston — we're still married because I could never get the money together for a divorce, but now —

MYRA.   *(Interrupting.)* What's your wife's name?

WILLIS.   Gladys.

MYRA.   Gladys what?

WILLIS.   Gladys Mayfield was her girlhood name, then Gladys Toome when she married me —

MYRA.   Is it Ashenback now?

WILLIS.   Well, that's the name of the man she left me for.

MYRA.   Well, I never.

WILLIS.   That's if they're still together and they were last I heard —

MYRA.   I got a postcard from her a week ago —

WILLIS.   You did? Do you know her?

MYRA.   Never heard of her before in my life.

WILLIS.   What did the postcard say?

MYRA.   "Keep away from my husband. I warn you." Gladys Ashenback. I said to Pete this must be a crazy woman. I don't know anybody named Gladys Ashenback.

WILLIS.   Well, I'll be switched.

MYRA.   So will you please tell her for me the next time you see her I'm not interested in her husband.

WILLIS.   Maybe she meant me — You see, like I said, we've never divorced.

MYRA.   Well, then, maybe she did.

WILLIS.   Well, she can just send all the postcards she wants, she will never get me back — *(A pause.)* I've told you what I think about you, Myra. What do you think about me?

MYRA.   I think you're very nice, too, Willis.

WILLIS.   If I get a divorce now, would you ever consider

marrying me?

MYRA. I might.

WILLIS. Would I have to get my house built first? I know a nice two bedroom apartment over at Mrs. Carver —

MYRA. Well, Willis —

WILLIS. Marry me, Myra, please. Please marry me. I'm very lonesome, Myra. I know I'm a Baptist and you're a Methodist, but I'll join the Methodist church if you wanted me to.

MYRA. Oh, I don't care about that at all, Willis. But I think you have to get a divorce first and then we'll talk of marriage — and, of course, I'll have to see how Pete feels about my marrying. *(Mrs. Jackson comes out of the house.)*

MRS. JACKSON. Oh, excuse me, Myra. I didn't realize you had company. Hello, Willis.

WILLIS. Hello, Mrs. Jackson.

MRS. JACKSON. Mr. Jackson is snoring so it woke me up. Did you hear him snoring?

MYRA. No.

WILLIS. I didn't either.

MRS. JACKSON. I'm surprised, he was snoring loud enough, I thought, to wake the dead — listen. *(A pause, we can hear snoring.)* I swear, Gabriel won't need a trumpet on resurrection morning, I tell him, they'll just have to get you to snore. *(A pause.)* It's so warm in the house — cool out here. *(A pause.)* What time is it?

WILLIS. Eleven.

MRS. JACKSON. Is it? I'll be dead tomorrow. You're a Baptist, Willis?

WILLIS. Yes.

MRS. JACKSON. We're all Methodists in this house. Except Mr. Jackson, I'm sorry to say. He belongs to no church, of course, he's the finest man I know — good and steady, no bad habits. Myra?

MYRA. Yes, Ma'am.

MRS. JACKSON. I have to speak with you about the girls' piano lessons. I know we talked of their studying with you in exchange for part of your rent, but with all the expenses facing us in moving after Mr. Jackson bumps another man, we can't afford to give up even part of the rent. I hope you don't mind and you haven't counted too much on it.

MYRA.   That's all right. I understand.

MRS. JACKSON.   Vesta's very disappointed and upset. She had her heart set on studying with you. *(A pause.)* Oh, I almost forgot to tell you there is a note for you by the phone, Myra. It's from Pete. He said to tell you he's spending the rest of the summer in Houston. He'll go to summer school there if he can. *(A pause.)*

MYRA.   Well, I'm going to say good night.

MRS. JACKSON.   Good night.

WILLIS.   Good night. *(Myra goes into her room.)*

MRS. JACKSON.   She's a very nice person. We often hear her crying in her room at night these last two weeks, but she's nice. That worries Mr. Jackson so. I think she gets upset from watching all those picture shows. A lot of them are sad, you know. Mr. Jackson says it is not picture shows worrying her, he says it's having to raise a boy alone on little money and now having to worry about maybe losing her job at the picture show. That's why we were all hoping Pete would come home soon — he's company for her. He's a nice boy —

WILLIS.   Yes, he is.

MRS. JACKSON.   Well, I think I'm going to bed and try to get to sleep. Good night. *(She goes into the house.)*

WILLIS.   Good night. *(He starts out of the yard as the light fades. The lights are brought up. It is the next day. Vesta is sitting on the porch doing her nails, her hair is in curlers. Estaquio Trevino, 17, a Mexican, comes into the yard.)*

ESTAQUIO.   *Buenos dias.*

VESTA.   What did you say?

ESTAQUIO.   *Buenos dias.* Good day — *Buenos dias.* That's Spanish for good day.

VESTA.   Well, you couldn't prove it by me.

ESTAQUIO.   *Buenos noches* is good night. Don't you study Spanish in school?

VESTA.   No.

ESTAQUIO.   I would think you would study Spanish being so close to Mexico and all. Texas used to belong to Mexico.

It was called *Tejas* then.

VESTA. Any fool knows that.

ESTAQUIO. I just a met a colored boy who didn't. He said I was making the whole thing up. I'm a preacher's son.

VESTA. My foot —

ESTAQUIO. I certainly am. We came here hoping to start a church. A Spanish speaking church. We hoped with the Mexicans in New Gulf and the Mexicans here there would be some interest. But we got discouraged very soon. There are plenty of Mexicans in New Gulf, but they are all Catholic.

VESTA. I thought all Mexicans were Catholic.

ESTAQUIO. No. Definitely not. There are plenty of Mexican Baptists and we're spreading the word. Do you have a sister?

VESTA. Yes. What's it to you?

ESTAQUIO. And her name is Katie Bell.

VESTA. Why?

ESTAQUIO. I've come to tell her goodbye.

VESTA. How do you know my sister?

ESTAQUIO. We exchanged greetings downtown the other day. *(Katie Bell comes in.)* Hello.

KATIE BELL. Hello. *(Vesta goes into the house.)* What are you doing here?

ESTAQUIO. I've come to say goodbye. I'm going back to Mexico.

KATIE BELL. Oh, well. Goodbye.

ESTAQUIO. And I've come to invite you to visit me in Mexico one day.

KATIE BELL. Thank you, but I wouldn't dare go there.

ESTAQUIO. Why?

KATIE BELL. It's too far away and besides, I wouldn't know a word anybody was saying.

ESTAQUIO. You could learn to speak Spanish —

KATIE BELL. I guess I could. I almost took it in school. I took Latin instead because Vesta did. Did you and your Papa get your church started?

ESTAQUIO. No.

KATIE BELL. I didn't ask the other day what kind of church

it was.

ESTAQUIO.   Baptist.

KATIE BELL.   We are all Methodists.

ESTAQUIO.   Are you? We Baptists believe in total immersion and we have no crosses in our church —

KATIE BELL.   Is that so?

ESTAQUIO.   I hope to be a preacher one day —

KATIE BELL.   Baptist?

ESTAQUIO.   Certainly — Jesus was a Baptist, you know —

KATIE BELL.   Was he?

ESTAQUIO.   Yes.

KATIE BELL.   I never knew that. When you preach are you going to preach in English or Spanish?

ESTAQUIO.   In Spanish. *Jehova es mi pastor, nada me faltara.*

KATIE BELL.   What does that mean?

ESTAQUIO.   The Lord is my Shepherd, I shall not want.

KATIE BELL.   Oh, go on — *(Pete comes into the yard. He is 14. He has a suitcase.)*

PETE.   Hello, Katie Bell.

KATIE BELL.   Hi.

PETE.   Is my Mom here?

KATIE BELL.   She's still at the picture show. *(Pete takes his suitcase into his room.)* His Mom and Daddy are divorced. She's a grass widow. Do you know what that means?

ESTAQUIO.   No. *(Pete comes out to them.)*

PETE.   I'm going to find my Mom.

KATIE BELL.   Bye Pete. *(Pete goes.)* Well, if you're a widow your husband is dead, but if you're a grass widow he's still alive.

ESTAQUIO.   My Papa may let me start preaching soon. I'm practicing now. My first sermon is going to be about sin. That's a terrible thing you know, sin is.

KATIE BELL.   Yes, I expect so —

ESTAQUIO.   Sin makes you drink and makes you gamble and go wrong. I wrestle with the devil all the time.

KATIE BELL.   Do you?

ESTAQUIO.   All the time. I talk rough to him. I tell him to go away and leave me alone. The devil got hold of my Mama,

26

you know.

KATIE BELL.   Did he?

ESTAQUIO.   Oh, yes. Got hold of her and wouldn't let her go. My Papa prayed and I prayed but he won out. She ran off and left Papa and me. She hated church. Hated the Bible. Hated hymns. Hated Jesus. That was just the devil making her say that. We don't know where Mama is. We saw her on the street one day in Mexico City, but when we went up to her she said she didn't even know who we were. She told us to go away and mind our own business. But we didn't listen to her. We stayed right there beside her on the street corner praying, and then we went on. She never was a true Baptist, Papa said. Not in her heart. She used to slip off and go to confession all the time. I'm going to pray. Bow your head. *Dios, dame valor para testificar a ésta muchacha y su familia la palabra de Dios. Y que sean vendicidos. Tambien por medio de tu vendicion, ellos logren sus metas. Te pido SEÑOR, que con ternura ella se fije en mi.* AMEN. Don't I pray good? Papa taught me to do that. What does your Papa do?

KATIE BELL.   He's an engineer. He's been bumped.

ESTAQUIO.   What does that mean?

KATIE BELL.   It means when you work for the railroad when someone who has more seniority than you do wants your job they can have it.

ESTAQUIO.   Is he out of a job?

KATIE BELL.   No, but now he has to bump someone and take their job.

ESTAQUIO.   Maybe he'll bump someone in Mexico.

KATIE BELL.   Oh, I don't think so. *(Mrs. Jackson comes out on the porch followed by Vesta.)*

MRS. JACKSON.   Come in the house now, Katie Bell.

KATIE BELL.   He's a preacher's son.

MRS. JACKSON.   Who is?

KATIE BELL.   That boy there. He and his Daddy came here to start a Mexican Baptist church.

MRS. JACKSON.   What kind of a Baptist church?

KATIE BELL.   Mexican. They do everything in Mexican. Preach and all. *(She turns to Estaquio.)* Is your Bible in Mexican, too?

ESTAQUIO. Yes.

MRS. JACKSON. Why, I never heard of such a thing.

VESTA. We have colored Methodist and Baptist churches — how many, Mama?

MRS. JACKSON. Oh, Lord. More than I can count.

KATIE BELL. Say to her what you said to me.

ESTAQUIO. *Jehova es mi pastor, nada me faltara.*

KATIE BELL. You know what that says?

VESTA. No, and you don't either.

KATIE BELL. I do, too. The Lord is my Shepherd and I shall not want —

MRS. JACKSON. Is that so? Mercy. Why, that's remarkable. *(Estaquio begins to sing "Rock of Ages.")*

ESTAQUIO. *(Singing.) "Roca de la eternidad, fuiste abierta tu por mi, semiescondedero fiel, so lo encuentro paz en ti, rico limpio manantial, en el cual lavado fui." (Mr. Jackson comes in.)*

MRS. JACKSON. Daddy, that was "Rock of Ages" in Mexican.

MR. JACKSON. Is that so. I thought I recognized the tune. You from Mexico?

ESTAQUIO. Yes.

MRS. JACKSON. His Daddy is a preacher.

ESTAQUIO. There are plenty of Mexicans across the tracks over there. They told my Daddy they're going to start a Mexican school.

MRS. JACKSON. Is that so? Have you heard that, Daddy?

MR. JACKSON. No.

MRS. JACKSON. We have a nice white school here, of course, and a colored school and now we'll have a Mexican school. Well —

MR. JACKSON. I wonder if there are any Mexican Methodists — *(Myra and Pete come in.)* Well, look who's home. When did you get here?

MYRA. He came in on the four o'clock bus. He wanted to take the train, Mr. Jackson, but it would have gotten him home too late.

MR. JACKSON. Oh, don't worry about hurting my feelings.

I don't own the railroads. I just work for them.

MRS. JACKSON.   But I worry a lot about it, Daddy. Now more people seem to me ride the bus — what'll happen to the trains if everybody starts riding the bus?

MR. JACKSON.   I don't know. I got enough to worry about without worrying about that. *(He goes inside.)*

MRS. JACKSON.   He does worry about it. He worries about it all the time. Only he says one day we could wake up and find there are no trains at all. But that's foolishness, of course. There will always be trains.

KATIE BELL.   Myra, Estaquio is Mexican. Estaquio, Myra plays the piano at the picture show and she says that Ramon Navarro, Lupe Velez, Antonio Moreno and Dolores Del Rio are Mexican. Do you know them?

ESTAQUIO.   Oh, yes. Very well. They're all Baptists.

MRS. JACKSON.   Is that so?

ESTAQUIO.   Just like Jesus.

MRS. JACKSON.   Oh —

ESTAQUIO.   Well, so very nice to have met you all. *(He leaves.)*

KATIE BELL.   Was there a good crowd at the picture show this afternoon?

MYRA.   Pretty fair.

KATIE BELL.   Is it still the Bessie Love picture?

MYRA.   No. Colleen Moore.

KATIE BELL.   She has one brown eye and one blue eye.

MYRA.   That's what they say.

MRS. JACKSON.   How do you know that, Katie Bell?

KATIE BELL.   Someone told me.

VESTA.   No one told you anything. You got it out of movie magazines. When she's down at the drug store she slips those movie magazines and reads them.

KATIE BELL.   I do not.

VESTA.   You do too. *(Willis comes in.)*

WILLIS.   Well, look who's home. Get your glove and let's play a game of catch.

PETE.   I don't want to play catch — *(He goes inside the house.)*

MYRA.   He's mad because he had to come home. Well, he'll

get over it. *(She goes inside.)*

VESTA.   His Daddy has a swimming pool in Houston, I guess he misses that — *(Mrs. Jackson goes into the house.)*

KATIE BELL.   Did you know Jesus was a Baptist?

VESTA.   That's a big lie — who told you that?

KATIE BELL.   That Mexican boy.

VESTA.   My foot. That's a big lie. *(Calling into the house.)* Mama, was Jesus a Baptist? *(Mrs. Jackson comes out on the porch.)*

MRS. JACKSON.   What?

VESTA.   You heard that Mexican boy tell her Jesus was a Baptist. Was he?

MRS. JACKSON.   Well, that don't make it so —

VESTA.   What was he, Mama?

MRS. JACKSON.   What was who?

VESTA.   Jesus — was he a Methodist?

MRS. JACKSON.   Well, now. I'm not sure — he could have been, of course. I don't know if it says in the Bible, do you Willis?

WILLIS.   What?

MRS. JACKSON.   What denomination Jesus was.

WILLIS.   I don't believe so. He was born a Jew.

VESTA.   Well, he's certainly not any Mexican Baptist. I know that. Tell that to your Mexican friend next time you see him — *(She goes into the house.)*

WILLIS.   I'm going to wash up. *(He goes. Mrs. Jackson and Katie Bell go inside. The lights are brought up in the bedroom Myra and Pete share. Pete is there with his glove and baseball. He is angrily throwing the ball into the glove over and over. Myra comes in. She gets a newspaper and tries to read, ignoring the noise of the ball as it hits the glove.)*

MYRA.   If you want to do that, Son, go outside.

PETE.   I don't want to go outside.

MYRA.   Let's both go outside, it's cooler out there.

PETE.   I don't want to go outside.

MYRA.   Come on.

PETE.   How many times do I have to tell you, Lady, I don't want to go outside.

MYRA.   All right, then. *(A pause.)* Your Daddy told me you'd been swimming in the river here. *(Pete doesn't answer. He continues to smack the ball into the glove.)* Did you hear my question, Pete?

PETE.   I heard it.

MYRA.   Is what your Daddy said true?

PETE.   I guess so.

MYRA.   You guess? Don't you know? Did you go swimming in that river?

PETE.   Yes. *(He stops throwing the ball into his glove.)*

MYRA.   How many times?

PETE.   Six or seven.

MYRA.   Pete, I told you not to do that, you promised me you wouldn't.

PETE.   What do you expect me to do — just sit around here in this room and rot.

MYRA.   I don't want you to go into a river that's dangerous and that has suckholes and alligators and poisonous snakes and where you could be drowned —

PETE.   A lot of boys go in the river.

MYRA.   I don't care what a lot of boys do. I don't want you to go. *(A pause.)* You hear me? *(A pause.)* Pete?

PETE.   What?

MYRA.   How do you like Willis?

PETE.   He's O.K.

MYRA.   He likes you.

PETE.   So?

MYRA.   He likes you a lot. *(Pete goes back to the ball and glove.)* Put the ball down, Son, it's making me very nervous. *(He does so.)* Pete …

PETE.   Yes?

MYRA.   He's asked me to marry him when he gets a divorce from his wife. *(A pause.)* How would you feel about that? *(Pete shrugs his shoulders, but says nothing.)* I told him I couldn't say I'd marry him until I talked it over with you first, I told him I couldn't marry anyone you didn't like. *(A pause.)* Do you like him? *(Again Pete shrugs his shoulders.)* Maybe if you could get to know him better you would get to like him. *(A pause.)* Pete, I'm at my wits end, Son. I promised you we would never move

31

again and I am going to keep my promise if it's humanly possible, but I don't know what I'll do if the picture show goes talkie, but if I married Willis we would live on here, he has money to buy a lot and build a house where you can have your own room. He's a nice man, Son, kind, he doesn't drink, he works hard and could support us — *(A pause.)*

PETE.   Mama?

MYRA.   Yes, Son.

PETE.   I feel terrible about this, Mama —

MYRA.   What about, Son?

PETE.   What I'm about to tell you.

MYRA.   What is it, Son?

PETE.   Well, you go ahead and marry Willis, if you want to Mama, but I don't want to live here anymore —

MYRA.   You don't?

PETE.   No.

MYRA.   Well, that makes everything different, then.

PETE.   Mama?

MYRA.   Yes, Son.

PETE.   This sure is hard for me to say, because it's not that I don't love you, because I do, but I don't want to live here with you anymore, Mama, or any place —

MYRA.   Now that's just your Daddy poisoning your mind. He has no right to —

PETE.   It's not Daddy, Mama. It's me. I almost ran off just now and hitchhiked back to Houston without saying anything, but I just couldn't do that, Mama. So please let me go back.

MYRA.   When?

PETE.   Tomorrow.

MYRA.   Tomorrow?

PETE.   Yes, Ma'am. *(A pause.)* You see, Mama, there's nothing for me to do here —

MYRA.   I know that.

PETE.   Dad said he will teach me to drive his truck and I can start to work for him in my spare time. They have a swimming pool and a car and a nice house and he's married to a nice lady.

MYRA.   Is she?

PETE.   Oh, very nice and I like my brothers. We all have a lot of fun together. *(A pause. Myra cries.)* Mama, please don't cry. I don't mean to make you cry. *(A pause. Myra wipes her eyes.)*

MYRA.   I know that. If I let you go will you come and spend your holidays with me?

PETE.   Sure. Are you gonna marry Willis?

MYRA.   I don't know.

PETE.   Dad said the other night he hoped you would get married again. He said you sure couldn't make a living any longer playing the picture shows.

MYRA.   When do you want to leave, Son?

PETE.   Tomorrow.

MYRA.   Tomorrow?

PETE.   Yes, Ma'am, if you don't mind. Dad is driving everybody to Colorado for a two week vacation and they all want me to go with them.

MYRA.   What about summer school?

PETE.   I'll catch up next summer.

MYRA.   Pete.

PETE.   Please, Mama. I want to go.

MYRA.   All right, then. *(She looks at her wristwatch.)* I have to go to work. Here's some money. Go on uptown and get something to eat later on.

PETE.   Yes, Ma'am.

MYRA.   I'll see you later, Son.

PETE.   All right.

MYRA.   And when you go to Houston tomorrow take the train instead of the bus, it would please Mr. Jackson.

PETE.   I don't have to take either, Dad is coming for me.

MYRA.   Oh. Bye, Son. *(She leaves him.)*

PETE.   Mama. *(Myra goes out of her room, into the living room and outside. Pete takes his glove and baseball and follows after her. When he gets to the yard he stops.)*

MYRA.   So long —

PETE.   So long — *(Myra continues. Pete throws the ball up in the air and catches it as the lights fade. The lights are brought up an hour later. Pete is still in the yard. Katie Bell comes to the door.)*

33

KATIE BELL.   Mama says if you'd like to have supper with us there's plenty.
PETE.   Thanks, I'd like to.
KATIE BELL.   We'll eat in about a half hour.
PETE.   Thanks. *(She goes as Willis comes over with his glove.)*
WILLIS.   Feel like a game of catch now?
PETE.   Sure.
WILLIS.   Gotta break in my new glove. Where'd you get yours?
PETE.   From my Daddy. *(They start to play catch. Gladys, Willis' wife comes in.)*
GLADYS.   Well, Willis — *(Willis looks up.)* Aren't you going to say hello?
WILLIS.   Hello.
GLADYS.   How have you been?
WILLIS.   All right. How have you been, Gladys?
GLADYS.   Tolerable. Who's your friend?
WILLIS.   He's Pete.
PETE.   Hello.
GLADYS.   You're Myra's boy, aren't you?
PETE.   Yes, Ma'am.
GLADYS.   I just bought a ticket to the picture show so I could get a look at her, but it was too dark in there and her back was turned so I couldn't see a thing. She plays the piano nicely though. Where do you live, Willis?
WILLIS.   Up there over that garage.
GLADYS.   Are you working?
WILLIS.   Yes.
GLADYS.   I'm miserable, Willis. Just miserable.
WILLIS.   I'm sorry to hear that, Gladys.
GLADYS.   Has Ashenback been around here?
WILLIS.   Not that I know of.
GLADYS.   Well, I'm warning you. He's liable to come with a gun, too. He's very jealous-hearted, he's very jealous of you ever since I told him I made a mistake in leaving you. I walked up to your girlfriend at the picture show, tapped her on the back and told her her game was up. She didn't even turn around and look at me if she heard me. She didn't miss a

34

note on that piano. I'm very tired, Willis. I've come a long way. Aren't you going to invite me up to your room?

WILLIS.   It's just a small room, Gladys.

GLADYS.   I don't care how small it is. Nothing could be smaller then the room we had when we first married. Do you remember that room, Willis?

WILLIS.   Yes.

GLADYS.   A regular closet. Ashenback is a four flusher, Willis. He talks big but it never comes to nothing.

WILLIS.   Is that so?

GLADYS.   Oh, my God, Willis. I made a mistake running off with him.

WILLIS.   Did you?

GLADYS.   Yes, I did. You know what he's doing now? He's a vendor for cigarette machines. That's how I heard about you and Myra. He said he looked you up the last time he was in Harrison and you proceeded to tell him about your girlfriend, Myra.

WILLIS.   He never looked me up.

GLADYS.   Ashenback is such a liar. He's lied since the first day I met him. Told me the first time I met him that he had a bank account of a hundred thousand dollars. And I believed him, too. And that's not the only lie of his I believed. We'd be here all night if I told you all the lies Ashenback has told me since we were together. *(Ashenback comes in.)* Ashenback, you are the biggest liar God ever made. Willis never told you nothing about a girlfriend. Did you, Willis?

WILLIS.   No.

ASHENBACK.   Never mind about that. His having a girlfriend wasn't a lie, was it? You don't always tell the truth yourself — You told me you were going to visit your Mama and when I called your Mama to see if you had gotten there, she said she hadn't heard a word from you in a month. But I wasn't born yesterday, I figured exactly where you had gone. *(He draws a gun.)* Keep away from Gladys, Mister.

WILLIS.   Are you crazy? I don't know what you are talking about. This is the first time I've seen Gladys in I don't know when.

GLADYS. Willis, don't let him intimidate you, he's all bluff. *(Katie Bell appears.)*

KATIE BELL. Supper, Pete.

PETE. I'll be along in a minute.

KATIE BELL. Who's your company?

GLADYS. I'm Willis' wife.

KATIE BELL. How do you do?

ASHENBACK. Come on home, Gladys. Don't cause me to commit murder.

GLADYS. You're all bluff.

ASHENBACK. Am I?

GLADYS. You sure are. *(Mrs. Jackson comes out.)*

MRS. JACKSON. Children, supper's on the table and getting cold. Who are these nice people, Willis?

GLADYS. I'm Willis' wife — *(Estaquio comes in with a Bible.)*

ESTAQUIO. Evening, everybody. *(He goes to Katie Bell and Mrs. Jackson.)* I have brought you a Spanish Bible.

MRS. JACKSON. Isn't that nice. I called Brother Meyers and told him about "Rock of Ages" being sung in Spanish. He was thrilled. He says there are Methodist Mexicans.

ESTAQUIO. Yes, Ma'am. Glad to hear it. *(Vesta comes out.)*

VESTA. Mama, the food is getting stone cold. *(She sees Estaquio.)*

MRS. JACKSON. Vesta, the Mexican boy brought us a Spanish Bible.

ESTAQUIO. Estaquio.

MRS. JACKSON. E S T —

ESTAQUIO. Estaquio.

MRS. JACKSON. *(Slowly.)* Estaquio. Would you read something to us from the Bible?

ESTAQUIO. Sure. *(He takes the Bible.)*

VESTA. Mama, our supper is getting cold.

MRS. JACKSON. Be quiet, Vesta, this is a chance of a lifetime.

ASHENBACK. Well, I'm not standing around here listening to any Mexican read the Bible. Come on Gladys. *(He grabs her.)*

GLADYS. *(Pulling away.)* I don't love you anymore. Leave me alone.

ASHENBACK. Gladys —

GLADYS. I don't love you and I never have. I love Willis and I always have and he loves me and I'm leaving you and going back to him.

WILLIS. Now look here —

ASHENBACK. Do you mean that, Gladys? Do you really mean you don't love me?

GLADYS. From the bottom of my heart, I mean that. You and Willis fight it out. I'm going up to his room. *(She walks out.)*

ASHENBACK. Gladys, wait. Please. Don't leave me. I'll kill myself if you do. *(He runs after her.)*

MRS. JACKSON. They're very upset, aren't they?

ESTAQUIO. Shall I read some —

MRS. JACKSON. If you will.

ESTAQUIO. *(Reading in Spanish.) En el principio creo Dios los cielos y la tierra. Y la tierra estaba desordenada y vacia, y las tinieblas estaban sobre la faz del abismo, ye le Espiritu de Dios se movia sobre la faz de las aguas.*

MRS. JACKSON. Isn't that interesting. What does all that mean?

ESTAQUIO. That's the first few verses of Genesis.

MRS. JACKSON. Is that right?

ESTAQUIO. *(Reading.)* In the beginning God created the heaven and the earth. *En el principio creo Dios los cielos y la tierra.* And the earth was without form and void. *Y la tierra estaba desordenada y vacia.* And darkness was upon the face of the deep. *Y las tinieblas estaban sobre la faz del abismo.* And the spirit of God moved upon the face of the waters. *Ye le Espiritu de Dios se movia sobre la faz de las aguas.*

MRS. JACKSON. Spirit of God? Do you know any other hymns in Spanish?

ESTAQUIO. Oh, yes.

MRS. JACKSON. "Blessed Assurance?"

ESTAQUIO. Oh, yes.

MRS. JACKSON. Would you sing that, please?

VESTA. Mama —

MRS. JACKSON. Oh, Vesta —

37

ESTAQUIO. *(Sings.)* "*En Jesu Cristo Martir De Paz. En Horas Negras De Tempestad. Grato Consuelo Felizidad. Nuevo Allento Al Corazon. Gloria Cantemos Al Redentor. Que Por Nosotros Quiso Morir.*" *(A gun is fired offstage. A woman screams. Gladys comes running in.)*

GLADYS. Oh, Willis. Come quick. Ashenback has shot himself. Somebody call a doctor. *(Vesta and Katie Bell scream. Willis goes running off to get to Ashenback.)*

MRS. JACKSON. Now keep calm girls. *(To Gladys.)* I'll call a doctor.

GLADYS. Thank you. *(Mrs. Jackson goes into the house. Gladys goes off as the lights fade.)*

ACT TWO

The lights are brought up. Later that night: Myra sits on the steps. Mrs. Jackson comes out in her robe.

MRS. JACKSON.   Willis and Pete not back from the hospital yet?

MYRA.   No.

MRS. JACKSON.   Oh, my heavens. I almost died myself when I heard that gun go off. Do you know what Mr. Ashenback's religious affiliation is?

MYRA.   No.

MRS. JACKSON.   I don't either, but I called Brother Meyers to stand by in case he's a Methodist and he's needed. Brother Meyers said he would go right over to the hospital in case he wanted someone to pray for him. *(Katie Bell and Vesta come out.)* Why in the world aren't you girls in bed asleep?

VESTA.   Who can sleep with all that has been going on?

KATIE BELL.   Where's that Bible Estaquio left, Mama?

MRS. JACKSON.   In my room.

VESTA.   I hope he doesn't make a practice of coming by here.

KATIE BELL.   How is he going to make a practice of coming by here if he is leaving for Mexico in the morning? *(Pete and Willis come in.)*

WILLIS.   He's going to live.

PETE.   He just shot his foot is all.

MRS. JACKSON.   That's a relief.

VESTA.   That can be dangerous — Cal Burton shot his foot to keep from going into the Army —

MRS. JACKSON.   Sister —

VESTA.   Well, he did. Everybody knows that and he developed gangrene and they had to amputate his leg. He had to use a wooden leg which swells when you get it wet and when he went to college and was taking a bath in his fraternity house, one of his fraternity brothers, a practical joker, used

39

to come into the bathroom and say it's Saturday night and you're supposed to wash all over and throw that wooden leg in the tub with him.

MRS. JACKSON.   Sister —

VESTA.   It's the truth, Mama, Thomas told me so.

MRS. JACKSON.   Well, don't be talking about such unlady-like things, it's not refined.

PETE.   I'm going to bed, good night. *(He starts in.)*

MRS. JACKSON.   In all the excitement you never did get your supper did you, Son?

PETE.   No, Ma'am.

MRS. JACKSON.   There's some cold chicken in the ice box.

PETE.   Thank you.

MRS. JACKSON.   I hear you're leaving in the morning, Son?

PETE.   Yes, Ma'am.

MRS. JACKSON.   We'll sure miss you.

PETE.   Yes, Ma'am.

VESTA.   Who do you look more like. Your Daddy or your Mama?

PETE.   I don't know. *(He exits.)*

VESTA.   Miss Myra. Who does he look more like. You or your ex-husband?

MYRA.   I don't know, Vesta. I'm not a good judge of things like that.

KATIE BELL.   Myra, tell her the story of that talking picture you saw in Houston with that colored man —

MYRA.   He wasn't colored, honey. He just put on black face when he sings —

KATIE BELL.   Why does he do that?

MYRA.   I don't know.

KATIE BELL.   Anyway, tell her the story.

MRS. JACKSON.   You better not start. We might get Vesta all upset again.

KATIE BELL.   Let her go in the house if it upsets her.

VESTA.   You go in the house. I'm not about to go into the house.

KATIE BELL.   Will it upset you if she sings the song?

VESTA.   No.

KATIE BELL. Sing the song to Mama, Myra, that the man sang in the picture show after his son died.

MRS. JACKSON. Was this a little colored boy?

KATIE BELL. No, Mama.

MRS. JACKSON. Oh, I thought you said the man was colored.

MYRA. No, Ma'am. He is a white man, but he puts on black face when he sings.

MRS. JACKSON. I wonder why he does that.

KATIE BELL. Nobody knows that, Mama, didn't you just hear Myra? Will you sing it for us, Myra?

MYRA. I'm sorry, honey. I just don't feel like singing now. *(She goes into the house.)*

KATIE BELL. Mama, if I tell you something will you not get mad at me?

MRS. JACKSON. Depends on what it is.

KATIE BELL. No. I'm not going to tell you.

MRS. JACKSON. Tell me. I won't get mad.

KATIE BELL. No matter what it is?

MRS. JACKSON. No.

KATIE BELL. Swear.

MRS. JACKSON. No, I won't swear. I promise, but I won't swear. What kind of language is that?

KATIE BELL. I went to a picture show once.

MRS. JACKSON. When?

KATIE BELL. Two years ago when I was visiting in El Campo.

VESTA. What did you see?

KATIE BELL. Clara Bow in *Rough House Rosie.*

VESTA. No, you didn't. You're just telling Mama that to get attention.

KATIE BELL. I did too. Are you mad at me, Mama?

MRS. JACKSON. No, not as long as you don't ever go again.

KATIE BELL. My conscience hurt me something terrible.

MRS. JACKSON. Of course, it did. Mine did, too, when I went to the medicine show and the tent show. Did you ask God to forgive you?

KATIE BELL. Yes, Ma'am. Every night for a month.

VESTA. Oh, rot.

KATIE BELL. I did, too.

VESTA. You don't even say your prayers at night.

KATIE BELL. I do, too.

VESTA. You do not. I hear you snoring as soon as the lights are turned off. *(Gladys comes in.)*

GLADYS. Willis?

WILLIS. Yes?

GLADYS. One of the nice doctors from the hospital drove me over here. I got me a room at the hotel but I left my suitcase here. I said you could drive me over to the hotel.

WILLIS. All right.

MRS. JACKSON. How's your husband?

GLADYS. He's not my husband. An ex-boyfriend.

VESTA. Is he going to lose his foot?

GLADYS. No, I don't think so. You know what he said to me, Willis, just before I left. He said he loved me as much as he did his God.

MRS. JACKSON. What is his religious affiliation?

GLADYS. Good Lord, Lady, I don't know. We never discussed religion.

MRS. JACKSON. Our Methodist minister, Brother Meyers, went over to see him in case he wanted prayer.

GLADYS. And you know what else he said to me, Willis? He said I love you too much to stand in the way of your happiness. I want you to do what you want. Tell Willis he has my blessing. Wasn't that sweet? Of course, like I told Ashenback, I said, Willis may not want me back.

WILLIS. Gladys?

GLADYS. Yes?

WILLIS. I don't want you back.

GLADYS. You don't?

WILLIS. No. I want a divorce now. I am going to marry someone else.

GLADYS. Myra?

WILLIS. If she'll have me.

GLADYS. Oh, I thought so. What a sneak she is. Moving next door to you taking advantage of you because you're lonely and missing me. Didn't you tell me when I left you you would never get over it? Never look at another woman as long as you lived!

WILLIS.   Yes, I did, but —

GLADYS.   Don't give me any buts, please. You men are all alike. Philanderers ...

MRS. JACKSON.   Vesta, you and Katie Bell come on in the house now. *(She and the girls go in.)*

GLADYS.   I have no money, I'm tired and I want to go to the hotel, but I have no money.

WILLIS.   Here's fifteen dollars —

GLADYS.   I can't walk into town with my suitcase.

WILLIS.   Come on, I'll take you. *(He picks up the suitcase. They start out. Mrs. Jackson comes to the door and watches. Vesta and Katie Bell join her at the door.)*

VESTA.   She's gone.

KATIE BELL.   And I hope she never comes back — *(They come outside.)*

VESTA.   Now, what do you think is going to happen Mama?

MRS. JACKSON.   About what?

VESTA.   You know. *(She points to Myra's room.)*

MRS. JACKSON.   Sh. Myra's in her room. She might hear you. *(Calling to Myra.)* Myra —

MYRA.   *(Calling from her room.)* Yes.

MRS. JACKSON.   *(Calling to Myra.)* Come on out and visit with us. *(Myra comes outside.)*

KATIE BELL.   Where's Pete?

MYRA.   He's gone to bed.

MRS. JACKSON.   I hope I'll get to meet Pete's father when he comes for him in the morning. It seems every time he comes here to see Pete, I'm gone.

VESTA.   Who taught you to play the piano, Myra?

MYRA.   A nice lady back in Nacogdoches, Miss Eppie Daughty.

VESTA.   Was she strict? Did she make you practice?

MYRA.   Yes she did. *(A pause.)* Did Willis leave with his wife?

MRS. JACKSON.   Yes. He took her to the hotel.

VESTA.   Did you know he was married?

43

MRS. JACKSON. Vesta!

MYRA. Yes I knew it. He told me when I first met him.

MRS. JACKSON. We'll miss Pete. He's been a lot of company.

KATIE BELL. I finished *Ben Hur* — I'm starting *The Four Horsemen* now. It says in the book it was a movie with Rudolph Valentino. Did you see that movie?

MYRA. Yes, I did.

KATIE BELL. Did you play for it?

MYRA. No, I hadn't begun to play the movie houses then. *(Ashenback comes in. His foot's bandaged.)*

ASHENBACK. Ladies. Do you know where Gladys went to?

MRS. JACKSON. She went to the Riverside Hotel, I think.

ASHENBACK. Thank you. I want to apologize for the scene I caused. Jealousy is a terrible thing and I'm infected with it. I can tell by your kind faces you've never been infected by jealousy. You should thank your Maker for that blessing. *(Mr. Jackson comes out.)*

MR. JACKSON. How do you do? I'm Ray Jackson.

ASHENBACK. Delbert Ashenback.

MR. JACKSON. You the fellow shot his foot?

ASHENBACK. Yes.

MR. JACKSON. Mama was telling me about it. You're lucky to be alive. Well, I hope you have that out of your system now.

ASHENBACK. I hope so.

MR. JACKSON. You certainly got everything fired up in this house. I'm usually asleep way before this, but I haven't been able to sleep. What doctor treated your foot, Vails or White?

ASHENBACK. White.

MR. JACKSON. Then your foot is going to be all right. Not that Dr. Vails isn't a perfectly competent doctor, but I have great faith in Doctor White.

ASHENBACK. Does Willis live up there over the garage?

MR. JACKSON. Yes, he does.

MRS. JACKSON. He's not there now, he drove that lady to the hotel.

ASHENBACK. I see, when you see him tell him I'm sorry for all the trouble I caused him. *(He starts out.)*

MR. JACKSON.   Will you be getting a room at the hotel too?

ASHENBACK.   No, I'm driving on home tonight, alone.

MR. JACKSON.   I see. *(Ashenback goes.)* I'm turning in. I think I'll sleep now. You coming, Mama?

MRS. JACKSON.   I think so. *(Mr. Jackson goes into the house.)* Come on girls.

VESTA.   Let us stay up a little longer, Mama.

KATIE BELL.   Please Mama.

MRS. JACKSON.   Will you get up in the morning the minute I call you?

VESTA.   Yes we will.

MRS. JACKSON.   Well, all right. This once. But don't ever think I'm going to let you do it again. *(She goes in.)*

KATIE BELL.   The time I went to Sister Pate's slumber party we stayed up until two. Some of the girls didn't go to sleep at all. But I couldn't stay awake after two. Rudolph Valentino died with appendicitis, didn't he?

MYRA.   Yes.

KATIE BELL.   There were headlines in all the Houston papers when he died, weren't there?

MYRA.   Yes.

VESTA.   Was he a Mexican?

MYRA.   No, Italian.

KATIE BELL.   He was 31 when he died. On the anniversary of his death, there appeared at his grave a mysterious lady with a long black veil. She told the reporters, she's coming back every year. Some say it's Pola Negri. Who do you think it is?

MYRA.   I don't know.

KATIE BELL.   Guess.

MYRA.   I just don't know — Wouldn't do me any good to guess — *(Willis comes in.)*

VESTA.   The man that shot his foot was here looking for you. He said he was sorry for all that had happened.

WILLIS.   Where is he now?

VESTA.   He said he was going back to his home.

KATIE BELL.   Without that lady.

VESTA.   I'm going to bed. You better come too, Katie Bell. *(They go in.)*

WILLIS. I'm really sorry for all that happened.

MYRA. I know you are.

WILLIS. I hope the Jacksons won't think any the less of me. I'll apologize to them tomorrow. I told Gladys I wanted a divorce so I could marry you. She said she'll fight me in every court in the land to keep me from getting a divorce. I said go ahead I don't care how long it takes I'm getting a divorce so I can marry Myra, if she'll have me. *(Pete comes outside.)*

MYRA. I thought you were asleep.

PETE. I'm too excited to sleep.

WILLIS. You're journey proud Pete.

PETE. I guess. Have you ever been to Colorado, Willis?

WILLIS. No.

MYRA. Ever since you've told me about Colorado I've been thinking about my Mama. She always said there were two places she wanted to go before she died — Colorado and California. Colorado in the summer time and California in the winter.

WILLIS. Did she ever get there?

MYRA. No, she never got out of Nacogdoches. *(A pause.)* I'm tired. I think I'm ready for bed. I bet I'll sleep sound tonight. Goodnight, Willis.

WILLIS. Goodnight.

MYRA. You better come to bed too, Son.

PETE. I can't get to sleep Mama, I'm too excited.

MYRA. You'll get to sleep — come on.

PETE. All right, goodnight. *(He goes into the house. Myra starts in.)*

WILLIS. Myra, what was your Mama's name? I never heard you say.

MYRA. Corinne.

WILLIS. Corinne?

MYRA. Yes, like Corinne Griffith, the movie star. My Mama died when I was sixteen.

WILLIS. Is Myra the name of a movie star?

MYRA. Not that I ever heard of.

WILLIS. I don't think Willis is either.

MYRA. No, I don't believe so. There is a Wallace, a Wallace

46

Berry, and there was a Wallace Reed.

WILLIS.   He's dead?

MYRA.   Yes. He died a dope fiend.

WILLIS.   My mother's name was Lena.

MYRA.   That's the name of a movie star — Lena Basquette.

WILLIS.   Is that so? I never heard of her. Myra, I'm really sorry for what happened.

MYRA.   I know you are.

WILLIS.   And I am going to get a divorce. I am — *(Pete comes out.)*

PETE.   Mama — I thought you were going to bed?

MYRA.   I'm on my way.

WILLIS.   Well, goodnight.

MYRA.   Goodnight. *(Willis leaves. Myra and Pete enter their room.)* Warm in our room?

PETE.   Like an oven.

MYRA.   Well, you'll be out of it soon. It's cool in Colorado. You sleep under blankets at night I'm told. *(She turns the lamp off as the lights fade. Next day — The lights are brought up. In Myra's room. Pete's bag is packed and waiting to be put into his father's car. Pete is in front of the house with his glove and ball. The Jacksons, dressed for a trip, come into the living room. Mrs. Jackson knocks on Myra's door.)*

MRS. JACKSON.   Myra — *(Myra comes to the door.)*

MYRA.   Yes?

MRS. JACKSON.   We're leaving for the day, Myra. We won't be back until late tonight.

MYRA.   You're going to look over Cuero?

MRS. JACKSON.   Yes, to see if we like it.

VESTA.   I think it's terrible of the railroad pulling something like this. Daddy has been an engineer for twenty-five years.

MR. JACKSON.   That's the system, Sister. I knew it when I started with the railroad. Seniority is everything. I always knew every time I went to a town I could be bumped and my job taken by someone who had been longer with the railroad. Mama knew that when she married me. I bumped somebody to get here.

MRS. JACKSON.   Only because you were bumped by somebody in the last town we lived in.

MR. JACKSON. And I can be bumped again, I guess, if someone with seniority wants my job there. Mama wants me to quit the railroad, but like I explained to her I've given twenty-five years of my life working there, I have benefits. Not every place gives you benefits.

MRS. JACKSON. That's true. He has a pension when he retires.

KATIE BELL. *(Cries.)* I don't want to leave Harrison. All my friends are here. Sally Doris said I could live with her until I finished school. *(Mr. Jackson exits.)*

VESTA. Oh, that would be just fine. Sally Doris! You'd be ruined forever living here with her.

KATIE BELL. Shut up, Vesta.

VESTA. Shut up, yourself. You'd be sneaking out to the picture show all the time just like you did in El Campo.

KATIE BELL. Vesta, you are mean. I told Mama I was sorry I did that.

MRS. JACKSON. Yes, she did, Vesta —

KATIE BELL. Can I stay on here, Mama?

MRS. JACKSON. No, you can't do that. We have to be together as a family. *(She and the girls go out to Pete in the yard.)* Pete, I expect you'll be gone by the time we get back. So we want to say goodbye to you.

PETE. Goodbye.

VESTA. When's your Daddy coming for you?

PETE. He was supposed to be here at twelve o'clock.

VESTA. It's two now.

PETE. I know that.

VESTA. Maybe he's not coming today.

PETE. No, he's coming. We're all going to Colorado tomorrow on a two week vacation.

VESTA. That's up in the mountains. Have you ever been on a mountain?

PETE. No, have you?

VESTA. No, and I don't care to. Laurie La Belle and her family drove out to Colorado and when they got there they took one look at those mountains standing up ahead and they scared them so, the very thought of taking a car up them things, that they turned right around and came home. Her Mama said, "no mountains for me. I was born where it was flat and I intend to die where it's flat."

KATIE BELL.   I'd like to see the mountains. I'm going to take Spanish in school next year so I can visit Mexico one day.

VESTA.   Is she, Mama?

MRS. JACKSON.   If she wants to. *(Mrs. Jackson goes back into the living room. The girls follow.)*

VESTA.   Are you going to let her go to Mexico?

MRS. JACKSON.   Well, that's a long way down the road. We'll see about that when the time comes.

VESTA.   If she goes to Mexico, are you going to let her see that Mexican Baptist man preach?

MRS. JACKSON.   No, if she goes to Mexico or anywhere, she'll go to the Methodist church just like she does here. *(Mr. Jackson enters.)*

KATIE BELL.   What if they don't have a Methodist church in Mexico? Can't I go to the Baptist church then?

MRS. JACKSON.   We'll talk about that when the time comes.

MR. JACKSON.   I'll talk about that right now. No child of mine is going to Mexico to be carried off by bandits and white slavers.

KATIE BELL.   Papa.

MR. JACKSON.   No and that settles that. *(He exits.)*

MRS. JACKSON.   Well, let's don't stand here arguing about Mexico. Let's go if we're going. Goodbye, Pete.

PETE.   Goodbye.

OTHERS.   Goodbye, Pete. Have a good time in Colorado … etc. … *(They go off. Myra sits in a chair.)*

PETE.   I wonder where Daddy is, Mama?

MYRA.   I don't know, Son. Something delayed him, I'm sure. He'll be along. Now I've packed your suitcase with paper, pencils, stamps, and envelopes. I want you to be sure to write me as soon as you get to Colorado. I'll be anxious to hear. *(The phone rings. Pete goes to answer it. She goes into the house and to the piano. She plays a Chopin etude. Pete comes back in.)* Was that your Daddy?

PETE. No. His wife. *(A pause.)* The trip's off. *(Myra stops playing.)*

MYRA. Why?

PETE. He's on a drunk and they had a fight and she says she won't go any place with him now or ever. She's mad.

MYRA. Oh, I expect she'll calm down. They'll probably call you tomorrow and say they're coming for you.

PETE. No, Mama I don't think so. She asked me if he had invited me to live with them and I said yes he had, and she said she can't have me living there. That she has two boys of her own to see to. She said Daddy is always saying things he shouldn't and putting his foot in it.

MYRA. I thought she knew you were going there to live?

PETE. I thought so, too, but I guess she didn't.

MYRA. I'm awfully sorry.

PETE. That's O.K. I'll go and unpack my clothes.

MYRA. I'll unpack them. *(Pete goes out. She goes into their room and begins to unpack the clothes. Estaquio comes in.)*

ESTAQUIO. Hi.

PETE. Hi.

ESTAQUIO. Is Katie Bell in?

PETE. No, she's gone for the day.

ESTAQUIO. Oh, well give her this will you? *(He hands him a sheet of paper.)* Tell her my Papa has decided not to go back to Mexico. He will stay and do missionary work trying to convert the Mexican Catholics to Baptists. He is preaching his first sermon this Sunday. All are invited, you too.

PETE. Thank you.

ESTAQUIO. Do you speak Spanish?

PETE. No.

ESTAQUIO. Then you probably won't enjoy it. It will be in Spanish. Tell Katie Bell I will be going to the Mexican school here next year.

PETE. All right.

ESTAQUIO. Are you a Baptist?

PETE. No, Methodist.

ESTAQUIO. Explain to me about the Methodists.

PETE. What do you want to know about them?

ESTAQUIO.   Their creed, what exactly do they believe?

PETE.   Oh, I don't know a whole lot about things like that.

ESTAQUIO.   Do you go to church?

PETE.   Not too often, Christmas, Easter ...

ESTAQUIO.   Then how do you know you're a Methodist?

PETE.   Because my mother told me I was. John Wesley was Methodist. I remember hearing that.

ESTAQUIO.   Who is John Wesley?

PETE.   I don't know exactly. I just remember hearing he was a famous Methodist. (*A man very drunk comes in. He is Gerard Anderson, Pete's father.*)

GERARD.   Pete?

PETE.   Yessir.

GERARD.   Who is your Mexican friend?

ESTAQUIO.   Estaquio. Estaquio Trevino.

GERARD.   Run on. I have to discuss personal matters with my son. (*Estaquio leaves.*) Did that old witch I'm married to call you?

PETE.   Yessir.

GERARD.   The Colorado trip is off because of that old witch. I said, all right. We won't go to Colorado, and I'm going to see my boy and tell him why. Tell him I'm married to the meanest white woman God ever created. Nag, nag, nag, all the time. Where's Myra?

PETE.   She's inside. (*He goes to the door and calls.*) Mama, Daddy is here.

GERARD.   How is your Mama?

PETE.   She's all right.

GERARD.   Has the picture show here gone talkie yet?

PETE.   No.

GERARD.   It will. My God. I've told and told her. There's no future in picture shows. Where are your suitcases, I've come to take you to Houston.

PETE.   Well, I don't know. Your wife says I can't come.

GERARD.   Did she? Well, hell, she'll get over that. Well, maybe I better not take you back today while she's still on the warpath. (*Myra comes out.*)

MYRA.   Hello, Gerard.

51

GERARD. Hello, Myra. How are you today?

MYRA. Pretty well.

GERARD. I'm in trouble myself. I tied one on last night and Jackie Kate pitched a fit. Called our trip to Colorado off. Did Pete tell you that?

MYRA. Yes.

GERARD. Well, hell, who was that Mexican boy I just saw here?

MYRA. He's a Baptist preacher's son.

PETE. A Mexican Baptist preacher.

GERARD. Well, hell, I don't care whose son he is. I don't want my boy associating with Mexicans. That's one reason I'm determined to have him live with me so I can teach him right from wrong. If they put in talking pictures here, what are you going to do? Look for another playing for silent pictures?

MYRA. I don't know.

GERARD. Give it all up. God Almighty — where are picture shows going to get you? I have a truck, a car, a beautiful house in a lovely part of Houston, a swimming pool, a wife and two lovely children and I didn't get that playing in no picture show. I got it by being practical in a practical world. *(A pause. He sways. He sits on the steps.)* Excuse me. I'm drunk. I'm very drunk. I beg your pardon. I have lots of troubles. I have to lie down for a while.

MYRA. Take him into our room, Pete. He can lie down on your bed. *(She goes into the living room.)*

PETE. Come on, Daddy. *(He takes him into the house and into the bedroom and helps him onto the bed. Willis comes in with his glove. Pete comes out.)*

WILLIS. I thought you were going to Houston today?

PETE. No, sir, not now. Our plans have changed.

WILLIS. I see. Who do you think is going to win the pennant in the Dixie League this year?

PETE. I don't know. Who do you think?

WILLIS. I think it is going to be a toss-up between Atlanta and Houston.

PETE. Did you ever see Houston play?

WILLIS. Yes.

PETE.   Who did you see them play?

WILLIS.   Atlanta.

PETE.   Who won?

WILLIS.   Atlanta. Want to play a game of catch?

PETE.   I don't mind. *(They begin their game.)* My Daddy is in there.

WILLIS.   Is he?

PETE.   Under the weather. That's why we're not going on our trip to Colorado. *(Myra comes out.)*

MYRA.   Pete, your father's wanted on the phone, see if you can rouse him.

PETE.   Yes'm. *(He goes inside and into the bedroom and begins to try and rouse his father.)*

WILLIS.   Hello, Myra.

MYRA.   Hello, Willis.

WILLIS.   Been warm today. A little cooler now.

MYRA.   Yes. *(A pause.)* Don't tell Pete, because I don't want to worry him. But Mr. Santos called me up this morning and said they decided they are not going to hold out any longer. They're going to put in a sound system right away.

WILLIS.   I'm sorry, what will you do now?

MYRA.   I don't know. I want to try to find a job here. *(Pete has awakened Gerard and leads him out to the phone.)*

WILLIS.   Don't despair — I learned that from my Mama. She used to say no matter how bad things look, Willis, we musn't despair. My Mama was a blessed woman. She had more than her share of troubles, God knows, but she never despaired. Never, never — as God is my witness she never despaired. *(Pete comes out.)*

MYRA.   Did you rouse him?

PETE.   Yes, Ma'am. Who wanted to talk to him?

MYRA.   His wife. She sounded very agitated.

WILLIS.   I'm moving out tonight. I'm staying with a friend I work with. Gladys is moving into my room. She spent the fifteen dollars I loaned her on clothes. The hotel won't let her stay on and I can't pay her bills there. *(Gerard enters.)*

GERARD.   Myra, I went to see that talking picture *The Singing Fool* because you recommended it. I thought it was awful.

I don't go to the motion pictures to be depressed. I like happy picture shows. Pete, who is your friend?

PETE. This is Willis. Willis, this is my Dad.

WILLIS. How do you do? *(They shake hands.)*

GERARD. I have to go back to Houston or there'll be no living with her whatsoever — she's on a real tear now. Accusing me now of being unfaithful with you, Myra. I guess the trip is really off now, Son.

PETE. Yessir.

GERARD. And I guess, too, I spoke too soon about your living with us. She said I had dreamed the whole thing up. I thought you liked the boy, I said. I do like him, she said, he's nice and polite, but our boys get jealous when I pay attention to him. She's just making all that up, of course, they are not jealous of anybody, she just changed her mind because she knew I wanted you there. Well, she may change her mind again. *(A pause. To Myra.)* I know you don't want my advice, but you're still an attractive woman. You should get married and have somebody take care of you. You're not getting any younger, you know. *(To Willis.)* Did you see that picture *The Singing Fool?*

WILLIS. No, I sure didn't.

GERARD. Don't waste your money. Unless you like being depressed. What was that song he sang after his boy died?

MYRA. "Sonny Boy."

GERARD. Oh, yes. How did it go?

MYRA. I don't remember.

GERARD. Jackie Kate said there ought to be a law against having picture shows like that that did nothing but get you upset and depressed. *(Gladys comes in. She carries a suitcase.)*

GLADYS. I thought you were coming for me in your car?

WILLIS. I said after supper, Gladys.

GLADYS. After whose supper — I ate mine an hour ago, not that I had much. A tuna fish sandwich and a Coke was all I could afford.

GERARD. How do you do? I'm Gerard Anderson. I'm Pete's father.

GLADYS. I'm Willis' wife. In name only it seems. He's smitten with somebody else.

GERARD.   Well, those things happen, unfortunately.

GLADYS.   Unfortunately. You still want a divorce, Willis?

WILLIS.   Yes.

GLADYS.   Well, you give me a thousand dollars and I'll give you one.

WILLIS.   I can't do that, Gladys. You know I can't afford that kind of money.

GLADYS.   You can't?

WILLIS.   No way in the world.

GLADYS.   Hell, I knew that before I asked you. What can you afford?

WILLIS.   Let me think about it?

GERARD.   Well, I'm going to have to go, folks. I have a long ride ahead of me.

GLADYS.   Where are you going?

GERARD.   Houston.

GLADYS.   Houston, oh, you lucky thing. Do you live there?

GERARD.   Yes, I do. I have a fine new brick house and swimming pool. Right in a lovely section of Houston.

GLADYS.   Oh, you lucky thing. How much can you afford, Willis?

WILLIS.   I'm thinking.

GLADYS.   Seven-fifty.

WILLIS.   Well …

GLADYS.   Five hundred, two-fifty —

WILLIS.   I could afford a hundred —

GERARD.   Well, I'll be seeing you, goodbye now. *(To Gladys.)* If you get to Houston look me up. Gerard Anderson, I'm in the phone book.

GLADYS.   Oh, I will.

GERARD.   So long everybody.

PETE.   Goodbye, Papa.

GERARD.   So long, Son. *(He leaves.)*

GLADYS.   When can you get me the hundred dollars, Willis?

WILLIS.   By the end of next week —

GLADYS.   All right. You sure you can't make it a hundred and fifty?

WILLIS.   No, I can't, Gladys.

GLADYS.   All right, will you take my suitcase up to your room for me?

WILLIS.   I will.

GLADYS.   Where are you staying?

WILLIS.   With a friend. *(He goes out. Gladys follows after him.)*

PETE.   If the Jacksons move and sell their house where will we live, Mama?

MYRA.   We'll find some place.

PETE.   Mama —

MYRA.   Yes, Son.

PETE.   What if you can't get a job?

MYRA.   I'll find something.

PETE.   Mama —

MYRA.   Yes, Son.

PETE.   I'm scared.

MYRA.   You musn't be, Son, we're going to be all right. *(She holds him.)* You're awfully disappointed about your Daddy, aren't you?

PETE.   Well. I knew it wouldn't work out. Nothing ever does.

MYRA.   Don't say that, Son.

PETE.   Does it?

MYRA.   Sometimes —

PETE.   What —

MYRA.   Well —

PETE.   What —

MYRA.   Some things have worked out.

PETE.   Name me one. *(Willis comes in.)*

WILLIS.   I'll be staying here tonight after all. Mr. Joplin loaned me twenty five dollars to give Gladys on that hundred I promised her. She doesn't want to stay here. She wants to take the bus on into Houston. She says she wants to start divorce proceedings in the morning. Well, I said, Gladys, I don't know if I can afford to give you your hundred dollars and start divorce proceedings at that same time. I may have to wait on that and save a little more money. Don't wait, she said, get the divorce first. You can pay me later. *(Gladys appears.)*

GLADYS.   Let's go.

WILLIS.   All right.

GLADYS.   So long, you all. *(She goes out — Willis follows as the lights fade. The lights are brought up a week later. Katie Bell is in the house sitting on the couch. She has the paper Estaquio left. It is "Rock of Ages" in Spanish. She is trying to learn the words. Vesta comes in. She sits beside her.)*

VESTA.   Is that a letter?

KATIE BELL.   No.

VESTA.   What is it?

KATIE BELL.   I'm not going to tell you.

VESTA.   Why?

KATIE BELL.   Because I don't want to.

VESTA.   Let me see it.

KATIE BELL.   No. *(Vesta tries to grab it out of Katie Bell's hand. Katie Bell goes out to the yard. Vesta goes offstage to the kitchen. Myra enters.)* You've been looking for a job?

MYRA.   Yes.

KATIE BELL.   Any luck?

MYRA.   No, not yet.

KATIE BELL.   We've had some good news.

MYRA.   What's that?

KATIE BELL.   The man that bumped Daddy to get his job, has changed his mind and he wants to stay where he is and so we can stay on here.

MYRA.   Oh, that is wonderful, Katie Bell. I am so happy for you. *(Vesta and Mrs. Jackson come out.)*

MRS. JACKSON.   Did Katie Bell tell you our news?

MYRA.   Yes, she did. I'm very happy for you.

VESTA.   And now Mama says I can take music lessons from you if you stay on here.

MYRA.   That's nice. I would like that.

VESTA.   Are you going to stay on?

MYRA.   If I can find work. I've no luck so far.

VESTA.   When may I start my lessons?

MYRA.   As soon as you want.

VESTA.   Oh, grand.

KATIE BELL.   Are you going to the opening of the talking pictures tonight?

MYRA. Yes, Willis is taking me.

KATIE BELL. I bet it will seem funny going there and not playing the piano.

MYRA. I expect it will.

MRS. JACKSON. What will happen if you don't find a job here?

MYRA. Then I will have to look for a job somewhere else. *(Pete comes in with books.)*

KATIE BELL. How is school? *(Pete starts for his room.)*

PETE. It's all right. I'm only taking one course. I wouldn't have to take that, if we hadn't had to change schools so many times. *(Myra follows Pete into the living room.)*

MYRA. It'll be behind you soon.

PETE. Did you find a job?

MYRA. No, not today —

KATIE BELL. We don't have to leave. Papa is not bumped any longer.

PETE. That's good. *(Myra goes out to the porch. Pete goes into his room.)*

VESTA. Could I have a lesson on the piano now?

MYRA. All right. Come on.

MRS. JACKSON. We'd better make some business arrangements first — will you still be willing to teach in exchange for part of your room rent?

MYRA. Yes. Thank you.

MRS. JACKSON. May Katie Bell and I watch the lessons?

MYRA. Oh, yes. *(Vesta and Myra go into the house and to the piano.)*

KATIE BELL. Mama, do you know what this is? *(She looks at the paper.)*

MRS. JACKSON. It doesn't look like anything I've ever seen.

KATIE BELL. It's "Rock of Ages" in Spanish. Estaquio gave me the words and I'm learning to sing it. Want to hear me? *(Starts to sing.)*

VESTA. *(Calling from living room.)* Mama, are you coming?

MRS. JACKSON. *(To Katie Bell.)* Maybe later. *(She goes inside. Katie Bell sits in the yard.)*

VESTA. I am so nervous.

MYRA. Now, don't be nervous. Now, you sit on the piano stool and I'll stand beside you. We'll start with some scales — now — let me explain the keyboard — This is middle C. *(Willis comes in.)*

WILLIS. Hi.

KATIE BELL. Hi, Myra is giving Vesta a music lesson.

WILLIS. I hear —

KATIE BELL. And I'm learning to sing "Rock of Ages" in Spanish. We don't have to leave Harrison after all.

WILLIS. You don't?

KATIE BELL. No.

WILLIS. Well, that's good news. *(Gladys and Gerard enter.)*

GLADYS. Hey there, Willis.

GERARD. Hello, Willis. Remember me?

WILLIS. Sure. How are you? *(Pete comes out of his room to his father.)*

GERARD. Hi, Son.

PETE. Hi.

GERARD. I have some news for you. Jackie Kate and I have decided to split up. And I've fallen in love with this lady here. You remember her, don't you?

PETE. Yessir.

GERARD. We're on our way to Mexico to get our divorces so we can marry. I just wanted to stop by and give you the news myself.

GLADYS. And it won't cost you a cent, Willis. Gerard's paying for the whole thing.

GERARD. Every penny.

GLADYS. The minute I laid eyes on him in this yard I knew we were made for each other. He said he felt the same way.

GERARD. Yes I did.

GLADYS. It was love at first sight.

GERARD. Yes it was.

GLADYS. Just like in the movies.

GERARD. Just like in the movies I like.

KATIE BELL. What kind of movies do you like?

GERARD. Happy ones.

GLADYS. That's the kind I like too.

KATIE BELL. What's your favorite one?

GLADYS. Oh I don't know. I like them all, as long as they have a happy ending.

GERARD. Tell your Mama to come out. *(Pete goes into his mother at the piano.)*

GLADYS. I called him the minute I got into Houston and he was all alone because his wife had gone off and left him.

GERARD. Took the boys, too. Said she was going to her Mama's in Louisiana and was never coming back.

GLADYS. And she meant it, too. When he called her and told her about wanting a divorce, she said go ahead and get it and see if she cared — so — *(Myra comes outside with Pete.)*

GERARD. Myra, I took Gladys to see that picture show you told me and Jackie Kate to go see and she didn't like it any more than we did.

GLADYS. Oh, no I couldn't stand it.

GERARD. Gladys says she doesn't think talking pictures will last, but I think she's wrong about that.

GLADYS. You do?

GERARD. Yes, I do.

GLADYS. Well, I just bet I am then, if you say so — Miss Myra, did you hear our news? We are going to Mexico so Gerard can divorce Jackie Kate and I can divorce Willis. Then we're going to Mexico City to be married. Isn't that just thrilling.

GERARD. Of course I'm having to give Jackie Kate everything I've got except my truck to get her consent. She gets the house, the car, the swimming pool. *(Mrs. Jackson and Vesta come out.)* Well, folks, we're going to have to be on our way. *(He goes to Pete.)* So long, Son. I'll send you a postcard from Mexico. *(He and Gladys start out.)* So long, everybody.

GLADYS. So long — *(They leave.)*

MRS. JACKSON. Now, who are they? I know I've seen them before but I can't place them.

WILLIS. That's my wife and Myra's ex-husband and they're going to Mexico to get a divorce so they can get married.

MRS. JACKSON. Why are they going to Mexico?

WILLIS. Because you can get a divorce there right away.

MRS. JACKSON. Oh. *(Train whistle.)*

VESTA. That's Papa's train right on time. He'll be here before we know it. Papa loves trains. He's said he loved them ever since he was a boy.

MRS. JACKSON. No wonder. He grew up in Palestine. All the Texas trains used to come through there. The L and N, the Southern Pacific, the Katy. He told me all he wanted ever to do in this world was to work for the railroad. He was working for the L and N when I first met him.

KATIE BELL. And he's never had a wreck.

MRS. JACKSON. No thank heavens. And I pray he never will. *(Estaquio comes in.)* Why, Vesta, there's that little Mexican preacher boy. Good afternoon, Son.

ESTAQUIO. Good afternoon —

MRS. JACKSON. Why, you're all out of breath.

ESTAQUIO. Yes Ma'am.

MRS. JACKSON. How's the church coming along?

ESTAQUIO. Not too well — thank you Ma'am. Nobody came.

MRS. JACKSON. Oh.

ESTAQUIO. So my Papa says we have to go back to Mexico. We're taking the bus to the border now.

MRS. JACKSON. Oh, I'm sorry to hear that.

KATIE BELL. I'm trying to learn "Rock of Ages" in Spanish. It's not easy. Would you like to hear me sing what I have learned?

ESTAQUIO. I don't have time. Our bus is leaving. If you ever get to Mexico, please look me up.

KATIE BELL. Where in Mexico?

ESTAQUIO. I don't know yet. I'll send you a postcard. *(He leaves.)*

MRS. JACKSON. Goodbye, Son.

ESTAQUIO. *(Calling from offstage.)* Goodbye —

KATIE BELL. So long. Everybody's going to Mexico. I wish I could go.

VESTA. You'll never get to Mexico, so you can just put that out of your head —

MRS. JACKSON. Willis, did you ever hear that young man

61

sing "Rock of Ages" in Spanish?

WILLIS. No.

MRS. JACKSON.   It was something. Wasn't it girls? *(She starts to sing "Rock of Ages.")* I'd better get supper started. *(She goes offstage into the kitchen.)*

WILLIS.   Want to play catch, Pete?

PETE.   After I finish studying — *(He starts for the house. Myra goes to him.)*

MYRA.   Pete —

PETE.   I'm all right. *(A pause.)* I guess I'm going to have a new step Mama.

MYRA.   I guess so.

PETE.   Maybe I'll try to find me a job here after school. *(He goes into the house.)*

KATIE BELL.   Are you all still going to the picture show tonight?

WILLIS.   I think so —

KATIE BELL.   Will you tell me the story tomorrow, Myra?

MYRA.   Yes, I will.

KATIE BELL.   I went by the picture show this afternoon. They were trying out the sound inside and you could hear it as you went by. *(Mr. Jackson comes in. He seems very dejected.)*

VESTA.   Papa, what is it? You look upset —

MR. JACKSON.   Where's your Mother?

VESTA.   Inside — what is it, Papa?

MR. JACKSON.   That fool engineer has changed his mind again and I'm being bumped after all.

VESTA.   Oh, Papa — *(Mr. Jackson goes in, the girls follow after him.)*

MYRA.   Oh, isn't that too bad?

WILLIS.   Well, maybe that engineer will change his mind again.

MYRA.   I hope he does.

WILLIS.   I hope Gerard and Gladys don't change their minds, and if they don't I'm going to be free next week to ask you to marry me. Will you marry me?

MYRA.   Yes I will. *(Katie Bell comes out of the house.)* How did your Mother take the news?

KATIE BELL.   She was upset at first, but she's all right. *(A pause.)* Myra, one of my friends said she saw Peter Pan with an actress named Betty Bronson. Did you see that?

MYRA.   Yes.

KATIE BELL.   And she said she has never heard of Betty Bronson since. And she wondered whatever became of her. And I told her I would ask you as you know all about the movies and movie stars.

MYRA.   Well, I'm sorry I don't know. *(Katie Bell begins trying to sing half to herself in Spanish "Rock of Ages." She finds the words difficult.)*

WILLIS.   Is that Spanish?

KATIE BELL.   Yes. "Rock of Ages." *(She continues singing half to herself, then pauses.)* Would you ever like to go to Mexico?

WILLIS.   Oh, I don't know.

MYRA.   *(Calling in to Pete.)* When you finish your studying, come sit with us, Son. It's cooler out here.

KATIE BELL.   How far is it to Mexico?

WILLIS.   Depending on where you're going. *(Katie Bell continues singing. Pete comes out and sits.)*

MYRA.   Get your studying done?

PETE.   I've got a little bit more.

WILLIS.   *(Pointing to Katie Bell.)* That's Spanish, Pete.

PETE.   I know.

KATIE BELL.   The name of the picture tonight is *Wonder* with Richard Barthelmes, Lila Lee, and Betty Compson.

MYRA.   I know. *(Katie Bell goes back to learning the words of "Rock of Ages.")*

PETE.   I'm going to go downtown and get something to eat.

MYRA.   Do you have any money?

PETE.   Yes. *(He leaves.)*

MYRA.   Well, I'd better get ready for tonight.

WILLIS.   I had too. *(They leave. Katie Bell continues to learn the words for a beat.)*

KATIE BELL.   I bet I get to Mexico one day. *(She continues the song as the lights fade.)*

PROPERTY LIST

Book, *Ben Hur* (KATIE BELL)
Popcorn (VESTA)
Stockings (MYRA)
Darning needle and thread (MYRA)
Sheet music (MYRA, KATIE BELL)
Lunch pail (MR. JACKSON)
Purse (MYRA)
Hat (MYRA)
Gloves (MYRA)
Nail file (VESTA)
Radio (KATIE BELL)
Hair curlers (VESTA)
Suitcases with clothes (PETE)
Baseball gloves (PETE, WILLIS)
Baseball (PETE)
Newspaper (MYRA, KATIE BELL)
Wristwatch (MYRA)
Gun (ASHENBACK)
Bible (ESTAQUIO)
Money (bills) (WILLIS)
Suitcase (GLADYS)
Piece of paper with Spanish hymn (ESTAQUIO,
    KATIE BELL)
School books (PETE)

SOUND EFFECTS

Classical music
Dance music
Chopin etude
Telephone ring
Train whistle

NEW
PLAYS

THE AFRICAN COMPANY PRESENTS RICHARD III
by Carlyle Brown

EDWARD ALBEE'S
FRAGMENTS and THE MARRIAGE PLAY

IMAGINARY LIFE
by Peter Parnell

MIXED EMOTIONS
by Richard Baer

THE SWAN
by Elizabeth Egloff

Write for information as to
availability
DRAMATISTS PLAY SERVICE, Inc.
440 Park Avenue South   New York, N.Y. 10016

NEW
PLAYS

THE LIGHTS
by Howard Korder

THE TRIUMPH OF LOVE
by James Magruder

LATER LIFE
by A.R. Gurney

THE LOMAN FAMILY PICNIC
by Donald Margulies

A PERFECT GANESH
by Terrence McNally

SPAIN
by Romulus Linney

Write for information as to
availability
DRAMATISTS PLAY SERVICE, Inc.
440 Park Avenue South   New York, N.Y. 10016

NEW
PLAYS

LONELY PLANET
by Steven Dietz

THE AMERICA PLAY
by Suzan-Lori Parks

THE FOURTH WALL
by A.R. Gurney

JULIE JOHNSON
by Wendy Hammond

FOUR DOGS AND A BONE
by John Patrick Shanley

DESDEMONA, A PLAY ABOUT A
HANDKERCHIEF
by Paula Vogel

*Write for information as to
availability*
DRAMATISTS PLAY SERVICE, Inc.
440 Park Avenue South   New York, N.Y. 10016